"There's a wide variety of [image] ut too few of these resources of [image] apply in their everyday lives. *52 Insights for Leading Your Ministry* is a testimony to Josh Denhart's legacy and experience, as well as his heart for ministry leaders around the world. This book will encourage you, challenge you, and empower you to take your ministry—and the people who serve alongside you in it—to the next level."

—Dr. Sam Chand, Leadership Architect, Consultant,
Author, and Speaker, www.samchand.com

"If you serve in ministry, you spend your days pouring into others—spiritually, emotionally, and physically. Josh Denhart understands the strain of shepherding children and families: that's why he's created a resource to encourage leaders like you to invest in yourself! Josh writes, "The more we pour into leaders, the healthier our ministry teams—and our ministries in general—will be." Allow this book to be a resource that God uses to refresh and renew you, so that you can serve even more effectively in your leadership role."

—Martijn van Tilborgh, CEO, Four Rivers Media,
www.fourriversmedia.com

"God uses Josh Denhart every time he speaks or produces resources for the ministry community. *Lead Volunteers* is a game-changer, and addresses the missing link in ministry: Volunteer Retention. Everything Josh produces is quality and comes from a pastor's heart. You should check out his resource."

—Ryan Frank, CEO, KidzMatter

"Josh Denhart does it again. *Lead Volunteers* is a vital and innovative resource for all ministry leaders serious about leading with a spirit of excellence. It's an indispensable ministry resource for anyone who leads a team, large or small. The tools given, if applied, will take your leadership and ministry to the next level."

—Esther Moreno, Children's Ministry Leader, Child's Heart Ministries

"Lead Volunteers is one of the most revolutionary and effective tools that has hit the local church in decades. Josh has perfected a system that will take your team to the highest level. I have licenses for all 10 of the church campuses I oversee. We got our money's worth from this investment on DAY ONE!"

—Brian Dollar, Pastor, Founder of High Voltage Kids Ministry

"Have you ever wished you had a children's ministry toolkit that had what you needed, when you needed it, as well as a trusted friend to provide input? That's what you get with *Lead Volunteers* and Josh Denhart. There's no better system for recruiting, training, and empowering your leaders on the market today."

—Mark Entzminger, Senior Director of Children's Ministries, General Council of the Assemblies of God

"What I like best about Josh Denhart's approach to ministry and ministry resources is that he has the mind of a leader and the heart of a pastor. This is evident in the Lead Volunteers program. It is clear that he will help you care for your people; and it's also clear that he wants to help you take your organization to the next level. *Lead Volunteers* is a 'must-have' for all ministry leaders!"

—Virgil Sierra, Senior Pastor, Vertical Church

"*Lead Volunteers* is one of the most innovative and powerful tools for ministry leadership I've come across in years. Josh Denhart is an incredibly gifted organizational leader with the ability not only to develop systems that maximize the effectiveness of recruiting, training, and retaining volunteers but also to clearly communicate the pathway for implementation. I am incredibly grateful for this resource!"

—Mike Howard, Lead Pastor, Revision Church

LEADV⬭LUNTEERS

MINISTRY INSIGHTS

52 INSIGHTS FOR LEADING
YOUR MINISTRY WELL

JOSH DENHART

FO
UR

CONTENTS

LEADERSHIP DEVELOPMENT

VOLUNTEER DEVELOPMENT

INTRODUCTION

I've been serving children and their families in ministry for many years; and one of the most essential truths I've learned in that time is that leaders need to be invested in and built up. The more we pour into leaders, the healthier our ministry teams—and our ministries in general—will be.

This devotional guide is designed to do just that. With sections to help you grow spiritually, in excellence, as a leader, and as a manager of volunteers, *52 Insights for Leading Your Ministry* has a wide variety of insights and application questions to help take your ministry leadership to the next level and encourage you in your own personal walk with the Lord! I can't wait to see how you are encouraged, challenged, and motivated through the topics in this book.

Each entry has a relevant teaching, practical application ideas, and stories from my journey in ministry. Following the entry, you'll be asked one or more application questions to help you apply the truths to your own ministry experience. Be sure to give a good portion of your time to the questions, as this is the key to translating these ideas into a context that works most effectively for you!

Thank you for joining me on this journey. As one ministry leader to another, thank you—thank you for everything you do, and everything you are. Thank you for saying yes to the call; to humbly cleaning up toys and pouring into families, week after week after week. You're storing up treasures in heaven, and you're expanding the Kingdom of God—there's truly no higher calling than that.

Sincerely,
Josh Denhart

SPIRITUAL
TRUTH

1

AN INHERITANCE IN HEAVEN

As humans, we all respond to rewards. We're motivated both intrinsically and extrinsically. God is a God of rewards, and He understands this motivation of ours. That's why He has incentivized serving and sacrificing for the Kingdom of God. Often, we need to be reminded about the importance of laying up invisible treasures in heaven.

What if you were to come up to a volunteer this weekend and remind them of Hebrews 6:10: "God is not unjust so as to forget their work and the love in which they are showing, in His name, while serving the saints"? A simple reminder like this can be wind in the sails of a weary team member. I advise you to implement what I call "2-Minute Tips" as part of your ministry: These short times are opportunities for you as a leader to continually pour into those who serve with you in simple ways. Remind volunteers why we do what we do, and the reward for doing it. As ministry leaders, we are the most consistent reminders of Scripture's promises to our teams.

As leaders, we need to be inspiring the people who follow us.

Do a quick Google search of Scriptures that promise rewards in heaven. Place these promises on a notecard and recite them on Sunday morning to volunteers. Remind them that service matters to God, and that He rewards us when we obediently serve Him.

1 Corinthians 15:58 reminds us that, "Nothing that you do in the Lord is in vain." We are fickle people who need to be reminded of this truth. As leaders, it's our calling to inspire and encourage the people who follow us. Remember these promises, and remind your volunteers that there is an inheritance stored up in heaven for them.

TAKEAWAY

Spend a few minutes looking up Scripture passages that talk about the heavenly rewards promised to believers who serve. Write below the ones that you think would encourage and motivate your team to keep fighting the good fight. Circle one verse that you think is the best choice to share with them this upcoming weekend.

Rejoice and be glad for your reward in heaven is great. Matt 5:12

I press on toward the goal for the prize of the upward call of God in Christ Jesus Phil 3:14

Now he who plants and he who waters are one; but each will receive reward according to his own labor 1 Cor 3:8

For our citizenship is in heaven Phil 3:20

2

ASK GOD: HE GIVES GENEROUSLY

Are you good with handling detailed paperwork? What about keeping up with current, complicated tax laws? I am neither, and so the responsibility of filing my taxes gets outsourced to a professional. Years ago, I called my tax guy with a simple question. One week later, I received an invoice in the mail. A half-hour conversation about an item that really wasn't that important cost me $80! Initially, I was taken aback by this; but later, in a calmer state of mind, I came to realize that tax professionals are paid for their knowledge. I had stepped into a relation-ship to gain knowledge from this person, and he *should* be paid for providing it. Now, I think long and hard before making any calls to my tax person. I go to great lengths, including doing my own research, to not be penalized financially for asking a simple question.

This experience with my tax professional deeply influenced my spiritual life. The writer of James shows God in stark contrast to this type of business. God knows that we lack wisdom. He doesn't shame us for this, and doesn't find fault with us. He doesn't charge us when He provides wisdom, either! We don't need to hesi-tate to ask God for spiritual wisdom—He is ready to provide it. With God, I don't need to try to figure it out on my own for fear of looking like an idiot. God gives generously to all without finding fault. He gives spiritual wisdom freely. He simply wants us to ask with faith and not doubt. God humbly says to us, "When you lack wisdom, please just ask. I am not going to charge you."

God gives generously to all without finding fault. He gives spiritual wisdom freely.

Whatever you are up against today, I want to encourage you to simply ask God for wisdom. Take the time right now and present your requests to Him.

If you are struggling with how to interact with a senior leader, ask God. Maybe you have a challenging volunteer you don't know how to engage. Ask God. When you're just not sure how to reach your kids with your woefully inadequate budget, ask God. If you lack knowledge regarding how to get parents engaged in the spiritual lives of their own children, ask God. He gives generously to all without finding fault. Remember, at the end of the day, God does not charge you. He does not find fault in you. He gives generously to all. God simply wants you to ask Him.

TAKEAWAY

What's one specific area in which you need to ask God for wisdom right now? Spend a few minutes writing a short prayer, thanking God for freely giving wisdom, and asking for His guidance in this area.

_____

_____

_____

_____

_____

_____

_____

_____

_____

_____

_____

_____

_____

_____

3

BE HUMBLE

James 4:6 states, "God is opposed to the proud but gives grace to the humble." This verse is extremely eye-opening: to think that the Almighty God of the universe could be opposed to me is very sobering.

I don't want God to be opposed to me—that sounds horrible! However, I often find myself migrating toward a position of pride, as we all can. I find myself thinking I can conquer this life on my own, and that I have enough human ingenuity to solve my problems, or make things happen. That's precisely what pride is—it's thinking that I can handle this by myself. Pride has a layer of self-confidence that is not only offensive to God, but is also off-putting to others.

I've been around individuals who exude a prideful spirit, and it isn't appealing. In the same way, I reflect on my past; the times when people have been less inclined to be around me were the same times I had migrated to a position of pride.

It is possible to lead confidently, yet under an umbrella of Christ-like humility.

The verse goes on to say that God gives grace to the humble. If God is opposed to the proud, He gives unmerited, undeserved favor to those who are humble. That sounds so appealing, so wonderful—and the path toward receiving this favor is a posture of humility.

As a leader, it's often far too easy to convince yourself that everyone needs to follow and listen to you. We can think that the greatest power comes from having all the answers. It is possible to lead confidently, yet under an umbrella of Christ-like humility.

I've lead from a position of pride, and it doesn't feel good. It's as if I've stepped out from under the protective umbrella of God's grace. Operating in humility means that you are tentative as a leader; you are not definitive. You are subject to change, new inputs, and new influences. A prideful leader, on the other hand, is so convinced of their position that they will defend it at all costs.

I certainly don't have the corner of the market on all the answers. That's why I surround myself with a team. I want to grow in the pathway of humility, for it is the path of unmerited favor from God. Be humble.

TAKEAWAY

Why do you think the Bible makes a point of telling us that God is opposed to the proud? What about pride offends, or disrespects, God?

_____

_____

_____

_____

_____

_____

_____

_____

_____

_____

_____

_____

_____

_____

4

DO NOT GROW WEARY

Paul wrote the book of Galatians to an agrarian culture—the primary livelihood of his readers was farming. This is why he says to them in Galatians 6:9-10, "And let us not grow weary of doing good, for in due season we will reap, if we do not give up. So then, as we have opportunity, let us do good to everyone, and especially to those who were of the household of faith."

God relates the laws of farming to the law of His Kingdom. Whatever someone sows, that will he also reap. When I begin to feel weary—when I begin to think that all of this might not be worth it—I need to consider this law. What I put into the ground it will come back. What I put into the ground will either bless me or burn me.

God is not mocked. He has set up the universe, both physically and spiritually, with a simple and straightforward formula: You reap what you sow.

It takes willpower to believe that the hard work I'm doing now will result in something of worth and value in years to come.

At any given moment, I can easily be overwhelmed and become weary. This is a journey of faith, to be accomplished with eyes of faith. It takes willpower to believe that the hard work I'm doing now will result in something of worth and value in years to come. It will take willpower and faith for you, too. Don't give up—keep in mind the abundance that will come with the harvest.

Finish strong. Finish faithfully. Show up. Give the extra time. Add another stone to the foundation of your ministry's future. Do not grow weary. It is worth it, even before you reap the benefits. You are doing meaningful work.

TAKEAWAY

What's one positive thing you're sowing in your ministry right now that will reap a harvest of blessing later on? What's one negative thing you're sowing that you want to stop sowing?

_____

_____

_____

_____

_____

_____

_____

_____

_____

_____

_____

_____

_____

_____

_____

_____

_____

_____

_____

5

DOMINATE WITH DILIGENCE

The Bible says in Proverbs 6:6, "Go to the ant, you sluggard; consider its ways and be wise! It has no commander no overseer or ruler, yet it stores its provisions in summer and gathers its food at harvest."

The ant is an interesting creature. Truly, it doesn't have a boss lording over it with a whip and a bullhorn, demanding that it work harder. Instead, the ant has, as part of its constitution and DNA, an *ethic* of diligence. The ant is referred to many times in Scripture, and is viewed as an excellent, commendable being. It works in the summer, and does not sleep during the harvest. The ant is constantly on the move.

Now, I'm not advocating that we working ourselves to the bone. What I *am* advocating is being diligent, efficient, strategic with your moves. We need to make things happen.

**We should be quick to work, quick to execute,
and efficient in our movements.**

There is a level of positive activity that is associated with the ant. We should be aggressive and assertive with our time on the clock, as well. We should be quick to work, quick to execute, and efficient in our movements. We should be creating processes, systems, and plans, and diligently setting them up.

Do extra work. If you think about a sloth—that crazy-looking, three-toed animal that sits in a tree for the majority of its life, it's almost comedic how slow the creature moves. Contrast that with an ant, who's busy moving and making things happen. Be the ant, not the sloth. Dominate with diligence.

TAKEAWAY

What's one way that you can be more efficient with your daily time? What's one strategy you can implement to maximize your effectiveness?

_____

_____

_____

_____

_____

_____

_____

_____

_____

_____

_____

_____

_____

_____

_____

_____

_____

_____

_____

_____

_____

_____

6

GOD'S WORD IS GRIPPING

One of the most important things we can be passionate about is the communication of God's Word. Of all the tasks we have—of all the duties and responsibilities in our ministry—we can never allow the beauty of God's Word to take a secondary place to anything...not order, organization, volunteers, or even system-wide excellence. The most important thing will always be the communication of the gospel.

We should place a significant amount of energy and investment into ensuring that God's Word is communicated in a fun, clear, concise, and memorable way. I've found that there are several types of leaders: some are purely administrative, while others are purely communicative. Sometimes, one individual can be skilled in both areas. Typically, though, a leader is either administratively gifted or gifted as a communicator.

**Clearly communicating God's Word in an exciting
and impassioned way requires preparation.**

Let's look at administrative leaders first. If you're gifted administratively, you'll need to find someone to partner with you in ministry who is skilled at communication. Find someone who is comfortable on the stage—someone who's vociferous, talkative, and animated.

If you are a gifted communicator, you might be prone to "winging it." I urge you not to get into this practice. Though you can stand up at any given moment and articulate yourself well, clearly communicating God's Word in an exciting and impassioned way requires preparation. Your typical extrovert communicator is prone to assume that they're capable of operating with little to no preparation. The reality is that those who are naturally gifted will be surpassed by those who put in the time and work to increase their skills. You will be surpassed if you rely only on raw gifting.

My encouragement to you, if you are a dynamic verbal communicator, is to sit down and map out where you are going, and specifically how you plan to land the airplane of your message. I've seen gifted communicators who lack the skill of *ending* their talk. I like to talk, and it's difficult for me to know how to end my message. You may just need an administratively-gifted leader to come alongside you and help you where you're weak!

The bottom line is this: learn to communicate God's Word in a clear, fun, and concise way. God's Word is gripping. Share it with passion.

TAKEAWAY

Are you an administratively-gifted or communicatively-gifted leader? Do you know a leader in your ministry who has the opposite gifting? How can you partner with this person to hone both of your strengths, and improve upon your weaknesses?

_____

_____

_____

_____

_____

_____

_____

_____

_____

_____

7

HOW ARE YOU SPENDING YOUR ONE AND ONLY LIFE?

How are you spending your one and only life? Eternity is a long time.

Years ago, our country was split into two parts: the North and the South. Imagine if an individual living in the South knew for a fact that the South would lose the war. He knows that a new era is coming, and Confederate dollars would soon be utterly irrelevant. Imagine that this individual lives on the northern side of the Confederate states—quite close to the border. In an effort to prepare for the future, he would be wise to make trips north, exchanging his current dollars into Union dollars. He would need to realize that his Confederate riches wouldn't amount to true wealth at all, and systematically transition those dollars into a currency that would last in the new era.

In the same way, wouldn't it be wise if we understood that the money, time, and resources we have in this life are spent exclusively on earth? We would be fools to not think ahead to our future reward. How are you spending your life? It's rather scary, but also inspiring, to consider that we have one life to live. We don't get a re-do. We don't get second chances. One shot is all we are given. The question we should be asking ourselves is, "Am I spending my one and only life in a way that reflects the reward I desire to have forever?"

The quality of our eternity is dependent on how we spend our one and only life right now.

Eternity is a long, long time—so long, in fact, that when we put our minds towards the concept of it, we can actually freak out a little bit. As a person of faith, I need to remember that this current life is the work zone that will influence the reward I will experience (or not experience) forever.

Knowing this, if we are aware that eternity is coming, and the quality of our eternity is dependent on how we spend our one life now, wouldn't we be compelled to spend it in a very thoughtful way?

We need to view our life as an opportunity to lay up treasure in heaven. Are you spending this life on Kingdom values, or are you stockpiling the things of this earth? Will you spend your life as a minister of the gospel, taking a road that is less traveled? If you choose to do so, be confident that you're laying up treasure that will not rust or be destroyed—a treasure that will be yours for all eternity. Remember, eternity is a long time.

TAKEAWAY

How does it make you feel to contemplate the reality of eternity? Does this contemplation change your perspective on your day-to-day lifestyle and choices? If so, how?

_____

_____

_____

_____

_____

_____

_____

_____

_____

_____

_____

_____

8

OVERCOMING SPIRITUAL PARALYSIS

Have you ever had a feeling of spiritual paralysis? I have—it feels like I'm stuck; like something is wrong. It was as if I had somehow gotten out of step with the Lord. Because of this experience, however, I have learned some of the key ways to overcome spiritual paralysis.

First, I ask God to search me, to know my heart, and to see if there is any offensive way within me (Psalm 139:23-24). Unconfessed sin will act as a barrier in your relationship with God. I record the convictions that I sense Him drawing my attention to as a result of my prayer. These sins may include shortcomings in me like a judgmental heart, a sharp tongue, a wrong thought, a wandering eye, or a prideful spirit. Now, I have a list of items to confess.

I mark some as "things," and others as "things to do." Some items weighing on my heart are merely things that I need to acknowledge—things that are bothering me. I cannot DO much of anything, for example, about my nagging cold. However, when I have a giant stack of papers on my desk, that is a thing to do—I can take action to solve that problem. "Things" are items I cannot control, and "things to do" are items over which I do have control.

Stress often comes not from what we are doing, but from what we think we should be doing.

It's good to remember that I can be in a funk, and yet that doesn't necessarily mean it's due to sin in my life. Separating these ideas has been massively freeing to me. My stack of papers (a thing to do) and my sharp tongue (sin), are not the same. Both are adding to my sense of spiritual paralysis, but their causes and remedies are wholly different.

Once I have my list, I pray and confess my sin. I clear up any unaddressed matters with the Lord. I leave them at the cross. I pray through the "things" list, the items I cannot control, and cast my anxieties upon Him, because He cares for me (1 Peter 5:7). I move forward, knowing I have entrusted my cares to God, and knowing that He heard me. I now pray about the "things to do" list, over which I *do* have control. I ask God to empower me to accomplish these things.

Rather than sitting and wallowing in my feeling of paralysis, I can pray, get perspective, and *get moving*. Stress often comes not from what we are *doing*, but from what we *think* we should be doing!

It's been a great blessing to identify the things in my life that need to be confessed; the items that I just need to talk to God about; and the items I need to get moving on. Try it out for yourself—this simple exercise very well may help you in overcoming spiritual paralysis!

TAKEAWAY

Write down both a list of "Things" and a list of "Things To Do" that you want to bring before God—they can be sins you need to repent of, items that are troubling you, or just topics you want to speak to Him about. Spend time going over each list item and surrendering yourself to Him.

_____

_____

_____

_____

_____

_____

_____

_____

9

THE GIFT OF SABBATH

Galatians 6:6 says, "Do not grow weary in doing good..." Part of mastering this principle is exercising God's provision for rest. The Sabbath day should not be thought of as a punitive command. It's not God's intention to burden us with the Sabbath. After all, he could have demanded seven days of work out of us.

Instead, according to His sovereign design and through His miraculous provision, He promised to give us seven days' worth of supply through six days of work. The Sabbath is actually a *gift* from God!

When thought of correctly, taking the Sabbath is an act of faith. Consider giving financially or tithing—in these acts of faith, we trust God to do more with the money we have left over than we alone could do with all 100%. In the same way, you and I need to trust God enough provide through our hands during six days of work, instead of foolishly thinking, "I can do more in seven."

May we never forget that the Israelites slogged through the desert, receiving double provision the day before the Sabbath, for decades! Those who sought to gather and hoard more, lacking faith and operating in "self provision" mindset, found that the extra they had gathered turned into worms and maggots: quite a lesson.

God knows our propensity toward self-reliance, our fixation on accomplishment; he knows the sickness that we will put ourselves through because of our own inability to trust and rest.

About fifteen years ago, I had a rather poignant wake-up call as I sought to do "catch-up tasks" on Sunday afternoons and evenings. What I found was that I was no further ahead, and yet I was struggling physically, mentally, emotionally and even spiritually, due to a racing mind and an overtly "American" perspective of accomplishment. After a powerful sermon on the gift of the Sabbath, some tears, some study, and some confession, I sought to shift toward accepting the gift of rest, and following God's example given to us on the seventh day of creation.

God knows our propensity toward self-reliance, our fixation on accomplishment; He knows the sickness that we will put ourselves through because of our own inability to trust and rest. I display my personal shortsightedness when I neglect the beautiful provision of the Sabbath as a gift from God. God desires physical rest and recharge for His people. We do not exist for the Sabbath. The Sabbath exists for us.

TAKEAWAY

What's currently holding you back from being able to fully enjoy and rest in your Sabbath? Is it not making space or time? Is it the worries on your mind? The pressure to always be doing more? Spend some time in prayer asking the Lord to reveal His truth to you, and empower you to rest well in His provision.

10

THE HAND OF THE DILIGENT WILL RULE

The book of Proverbs shares this wonderful statement that I think we all need to listen to deeply: "If you work with a diligent hand you will find yourself in charge. If you work with a slack hand you will be put to forced labor by others."

I don't know about you, but forced labor doesn't sound fun. It sounds a lot like doing someone else's bidding. I want to write my own ticket. The pathway to doing so in a ministry context—or in any context for that matter—is diligence. If you are diligent, and you work hard, you will find yourself calling the shots. However, if you slack off and do a pathetic job of executing, other people are going to become your overseers.

Now, what I've seen in the past from some in ministry is a whiny, cranky spirit when they are given tasks by their leaders. For example, I had a man come to me sad and upset once, wondering why he had been handed random tasks that had nothing to do with his ministry area—the senior leaders would come out of a meeting and hand things to him.

If you don't want to be told what to do all the time, be an individual who dominates with diligence.

After hearing him complain about this for some time, I had to have a hard talk with my friend. I shared with him, in all seriousness, that it was a matter of diligence. The senior leaders reviewed this individual and decided that he had plenty of margin on his hands. He had a lot of idle time. Because of this, he was seen as someone who could be tasked with more jobs. He was being forced to do those jobs—why? Because he worked with a slack hand. Because leaders will naturally delegate to someone who doesn't look busy.

On the other hand, I was not handed these random tasks, because I was diligently executing things, and had been for years. Leaders never thought to hand me random tasks, because they knew I was extraordinarily busy and had massive results to show for it.

The hand of the diligent will rule. I got to focus on the tasks that I wanted to do because of my repeated diligence. I worked hard, created new opportunities for myself, and executed those opportunities with care. At the end of the day, if you don't want to be told what to do all the time, be an individual who dominates with diligence, and you will find yourself calling your own shots.

TAKEAWAY

Why do you think diligence is one of the main qualities that leaders look for on their teams? How does diligence enhance your reputation with your supervisors?

_____

_____

_____

_____

_____

_____

_____

_____

_____

_____

_____

_____

_____

11

THE HARVEST IS PLENTIFUL

Matthew 9:37-38 says, "Then he said to his disciples, 'The harvest is plentiful, but the laborers are few; therefore pray earnestly to the Lord of the harvest to send out laborers into his harvest.'"

Have you ever felt buried under the pressure of your workload—specifically, the mountain of volunteers you need to find? What do you do when the numbers just aren't adding up? I must admit that, at times I haven't prayed and asked God for His help and leading. Often, I have taken on the task of recruiting apart from Jesus, instead of stopping to pray to the Lord of the harvest. My question to you is this: are you praying and asking God for more volunteers, or recruiting on your own?

In Matthew 9, Jesus says to ask the Lord of the harvest, the boss of the field, to send out workers to help. As soon as this was said, we enter a new chapter. Not only do we enter Matthew chapter 10, but we also enter into a brand new chapter in the ministry of Jesus. The Bible says in Matthew 10:1 that Jesus went away to a solitary place and prayed all night long. This is the time Jesus asks the Father which followers should become His exclusive disciples.

**Are you praying and asking God for more
volunteers, or recruiting on your own?**

The Bible says Jesus came down off of the mountain and chose the Twelve. This is so important—even Jesus specifically prayed to God to raise up the right people. He was praying for the men that would carry out and carry on the work after His crucifixion and resurrection.

Again, I ask: Are you praying to God for more volunteers, or trying to do the work of recruiting all on your own? We should not only follow Jesus's instruction, but also His example. You see, it's God's field. He cares about it far more than we do. Jesus gives us express permission here to ask for more people—more laborers!

He Himself went spent an entire night beseeching God for wisdom regarding whom He should pick. How much more should we do so? The harvest is plentiful, but the workers are few. There is no reason you need to take on this burden alone—ask the Lord of the harvest.

TAKEAWAY

Is there anything holding you back from asking God for help when it comes to recruiting volunteers and team members? Write a prayer asking Him to break down any defenses in your heart, and to send the best people to accomplish His purposes in your ministry.

_____

_____

_____

_____

_____

_____

_____

_____

_____

_____

_____

_____

_____

12

TO EXCEL AT LONGSUFFERING, ONE MUST SUFFER LONG

Perseverance and longsuffering are part of the ministry package. Leading in the ministry requires a hard labor of love each and every day. You'll encounter people who will intentionally, or unintentionally, seek to hurt and harm. It's important to know how to suffer these hurts and harms.

For instance, you are going to suffer the consequences of people not showing up to volunteer. You're going to realize the fickle nature of human beings. You're going to ask yourself the question, "Who does that? Who says they're going to do something and then doesn't do it—and doesn't *tell you* they're not going to do it?"

We will see the worst of people. We will see their flakiness and fragility in new ways. My job is harder because people don't do what they say they will. I can choose to be angry, bitter, and cynical about humans in general; or I can take up my cross and suffer. It may take energy and effort to understand how to work with faulty, frail people. But at the end of the day, if I am going to be good at longsuffering, I must suffer long.

**Ministry is a worthy and high calling.
Longsuffering is a beautiful thing.**

It's hard. It's hard to see the value of your ministry when others don't. It's hard to have your budget cut again, never to be replaced. It's hard to see your programs alienated and pushed to the side, not given the same level of platform or promotion as other programs. But ministry is a worthy and high calling. Longsuffering is a beautiful thing.

When others suffer long for me, it's truly a joy to see their heart and dedication. I have been the blessed recipient of other people suffering long as I try to pull myself together and make good on my word. People have suffered long with me, and I'm grateful that they have.

So let this encourage you—in order to be well adept at long suffering, we must first suffer long—and this is ultimately a privilege of partnering with God in ministry.

TAKEAWAY

In what ways has your ministry journey acquainted you with longsuffering? What specific challenges have you faced that have taught you a little of what Christ has suffered in His ministry?

_____

_____

_____

_____

_____

_____

_____

_____

_____

_____

_____

_____

_____

_____

_____

_____

13

THIS WHOLE THING IS ABOUT THE GOSPEL

Early in ministry, a wise leader warned me that the detail, disorder, and drama that come with the running a ministry can quickly eclipse the gospel from our focus. In reality, these secondary concerns should always take a backseat to the truth of God's Word that we're sharing with families.

The entire point of ministry—and, by extension—of recruiting ministry team members, is to further the gospel. The whole point of having a well-staffed nursery is to create an environment where young children have a deep sense of safety, that allows them to begin to understand God's love. The whole point of hosting outreach events is to create goodwill and share the good news. This whole thing is about the Gospel! Any gain that I seek to implement is for one purpose: to build relationships so that I can share the good news of Jesus Christ.

When I am laboring in the tedious minutia of an electronic check-in system that never seems to work, I need to remind myself that it is about the gospel. I'm doing this so that 21st century parents in a Western, suburban culture can feel a sense of safety as they drop their kids off. We live in a society where our perception of safety dominates everything. This, too, is building a bridge to ensure the gospel is not hindered.

Any gain that I seek to implement is for one purpose: to build relationships so that I can share the good news of Jesus Christ.

The gospel is our highest calling. If I can orient my ministry leadership to focus on the beauty and value of the gospel, then none of my labor is in vain.

Not only is our role to make certain that the Gospel is proclaimed, but it is also about our hearts. If I can keep my head above the waters of detail and drama, and set my eyes on things above, where Christ is seated at the right hand of God, I am going to find more joy and perseverance.

Remember, this whole thing is about the gospel—make it the focus of every single thing you do!

TAKEAWAY

What are some mundane, ordinary aspects of leading your ministry that you can begin to see through the lens of the God's Word? List them below, and take a few minutes to brainstorm how these tasks or responsibilities allow people to experience the love and truth of the gospel!

_____

_____

_____

_____

_____

_____

_____

_____

_____

_____

_____

_____

_____

_____

MINISTRY EXCELLENCE

14

AN ORDERLY MINISTRY IS MORE APPEALING

It's amazing to me the differences between an orderly ministry and a disorderly ministry. A ministry that is clean and clutter-free just seems more appealing.

To illustrate the difference, I have to take you back about ten or fifteen years ago, to a time when I was a high school chemistry teacher. I taught next to another teacher, whose room was identical to my own. We both had lab space as well as classroom space. I have a well-defined sense of OCD. I love order—in fact, I crave it. Therefore, my classroom was always extremely clean. I gave out extra credit to students who cleaned my glassware, wiped down my tables, and made sure my area was in complete order. Now, let's contrast this atmosphere with that of the classroom next door to me. This teacher had random chemical spills on tables, powders and liquids that were half-evaporated, and glassware stacked up by the back sink. There were messes all over her room.

Here's my philosophy: messy begets messy; cleanliness begets cleanliness. If a student in my chemistry classroom were to spill something, they would look at it in relationship to its surroundings, and notice that something was off. However, in the other chemistry teacher's classroom, if someone made a mess, it would blend right in. They wouldn't feel bad about leaving it there. Therefore, they would leave that mess.

If you have an orderly ministry, people will want to retain that order.

If you have an orderly ministry, people will want to retain that order. It's in their DNA. If you want to lead your volunteers in running an orderly ministry, *hand* them an orderly ministry.

Several years after teaching, I was children's pastor at a large church. A couple of times a year, the senior pastor would hijack a staff meeting and walk everyone around the building, pointing out things he didn't like. It was quite uncomfortable, especially for those in ministry who did not have a particularly high cleanliness ethic. It was embarrassing to have the senior pastor point out your disastrously dirty area. However, when they turned the corner into the children's ministry, by God's grace, we had a spotless area. We acquired a reputation for orderliness, cleanliness, and excellence. People wanted to be in our area.

There is a sense of calm in a clean space. The brain craves order. It seeks patterns and logical categories. It looks for efficiency. When it has to spend extra energy making sense of cluttered surroundings, it's a waste. I want my volunteers to serve in an area where the surroundings don't distract them—I want them to walk in and feel a sense of peace and order, so they can focus their energies on the ministry at hand. At the end of the day, an orderly ministry is more appealing — so clean up already!

TAKEAWAY

Think of a room or area of your ministry that's typically messy. What do you feel when you walk into that space? How do you think parents and families feel in this area? Now, think of an area that's pretty orderly and clean. What do you feel when you spend time in this area? What do you think families feel in this area?

_____

_____

_____

_____

_____

_____

_____

_____

15

BLOCKS DO NOT STACK THEMSELVES

God has created the universe in such a way that things move from order to disorder — from organization to chaos. It literally takes effort to build a ministry, just as it takes effort to build anything.

It takes energy to stack blocks on top of one another—this doesn't magically happen on its own. Blocks are far more likely to fall over than they are to magically stack themselves. Ministry takes work. If you're walking into a brand new ministry season, don't think for a moment that the changes and improvements you want to see are going to happen on their own.

If you want to reap the benefits of an orderly, systematic, well-oiled, and well-defined ministry, it's going to take work. No one will do it for you. I have seen many ministry leaders who have seen our ministry—what took our team a decade of diligent labor to create—and who have become frustrated and even angry. They want instant results, without understanding that there's no such thing. It took an immense amount of energy and intentionality to get things in our ministry to where they are now. You have to start someplace.

If you want to reap the benefits of an orderly, systematic, well-oiled, and well-defined ministry, it's going to take work.

My encouragement to you is to start with a healthy foundation. Begin with ministry processes and systems that others can easily stack upon. Sloppiness will lead to fallen blocks—chaos—disorder—messes you'll only have to clean up later. So take the time to lay the foundation correctly.

I want to spend time and energy creating a system that pays future dividends and stays in place long after I'm gone. That's the goal. A great leader creates processes and pathways that others can follow long after they are gone. Wouldn't that be a blessing to see in your ministry?

Blocks don't stack themselves. You have to give constant attention and care to the details. No matter the system you build, it's going to need human involvement and intentionality. Get in there, put one block on top of another, and understand that building a ministry takes work.

TAKEAWAY

What are some intentional steps you've already needed to take to lay a strong foundation for your ministry? What are some steps you haven't taken yet that will be fundamental to building a lasting legacy?

_____

_____

_____

_____

_____

_____

_____

_____

_____

_____

_____

_____

16

AUTOMATE EVERYTHING

I have a passion for automation—for setting up systems and processes that reduce human involvement and maximize ministry output.

For example, during my time in ministry, I kept an email folder called "Drafts." Inside this folder were 25 different responses to common questions: questions about baptism, infant dedication, our summer programming, and so on. These email responses were pre-written and well thought-out; they waited in the wings to be sent to people who had the appropriate questions. That is automation: working on something once in such a way that it works hundreds of times for me in the future.

In ministry, if we don't come to the table with some level of automation, we are going to be a small gear spinning so fast that it starts to smoke. That is a recipe for burnout. If you sit down and think through the elements of your ministry you can automate right now, you'll begin to set up a process that literally pays you back hundreds of hours in the future.

So, where do you start? Think about something in your ministry that is repeated. It could be baptisms, Easter services, and so on. Creating a process that automates all, or many, of the details surrounding these events, as well as follow-up, is an intelligent and important step to take.

Automating things means you put a little more time in on the front end, in order to see more payoff on the back end.

Every year, we have fall kickoff. It shouldn't be a surprise that we are starting things every September. An intelligent team would sit down and figure out all the items necessary for fall kickoff, and spend time fine-tuning and crafting each one.

After the team gets through that first year, we tweak it slightly, and then hand off some of the items to administrative assistants or even volunteers.

What does automation look like practically? Taking photographs of the fall festival display; labeling photos and boxes; having things stored and organized in an intuitive way, so that a volunteer who is hungry to serve can be handed a sheet of paper, directed to where the tubs are, and instructed on how to replicate what you have done in past years. Automating things means you put a little more time in on the front end, in order to see more payoff on the back end.

Think through what items are repeated weekly, monthly, quarterly, or annually, and seek to make repeatable processes for them. Automate everything.

TAKEAWAY

What processes in your ministry can be automated? What events, holidays, or special occasions can be prepared for in advance? Beside each that you list below, think of one or two practical aspects (emails, flyers, stage decorations, etc.) that you want to automate first.

_____

_____

_____

_____

_____

_____

_____

_____

_____

_____

17

DO WE BRING EXECUTION OR MERE ACTIVITY?

Years ago, there was a huge machine at the World's Fair. This machine had levers, and gears, and gave off smoke, in addition to making noise. It drew a lot of attention—people stood in amazement to see this contraption belching smoke, churning gears, and chugging away. Someone leaned over to the main engineer, who was standing proudly next to the machine, and asked a simple question: "What does this thing do?" To everyone's surprise, the engineer replied, "What do you mean, 'what does it do'? It just *runs.*"

Can this be said of your life? Is your life full of busyness, yet lacking real and meaningful results?

It's easy to get busy, moving to and fro between nonessential tasks—it gives us the feeling that we're actually accomplishing something. However, this movement itself isn't execution. I've seen too many leaders busy themselves with trivial matters, and gauge their level of execution based on their personal exhaustion. That's a terrible way to determine whether or not you have been successful. See, there is a difference between execution and activity.

Simply being busy does not mean that you are achieving anything.

One thing we often busy ourselves with in church culture is meetings. Meetings should bring about a list of items of things to execute. Many leaders view meetings as "work," but was anything actually accomplished in the meeting? I've sat in 7-8 hours of meetings in one day, and come to the conclusion that no real work was done. Simply being busy does not mean that you are achieving anything. A meeting for the sake of a meeting isn't productive. Instead, each hour of our work day should be devoted towards *achieving* something. Execution moves things forward, while mere activity is a waste of time.

Take a quick assessment of your work. Are you bringing execution to the table, or merely busyness?

TAKEAWAY

Can you think of 3 or 4 things in your current weekly routine that keep you busy, but don't significantly contribute to executing—getting things done? How might you alter these things to maximize their productivity?

_____

_____

_____

_____

_____

_____

_____

_____

_____

_____

_____

_____

_____

_____

_____

_____

18

SYSTEMS TAKE TIME, SYSTEMS MAKE TIME

Over the years, I've been guilty of spending an inordinate amount of time on the front end of a task or project. Instead of simply completing the task, I'll also create a system to make completing future tasks easier. As we've already discussed, automation is helpful for tasks that are going to be repeated or recurring ministry experiences. The secret to automation is creating systems! Not only do you need to document everything you do—you need to systematize it.

Earlier, I mentioned how I began to automate some recurring events, such as infant dedications. Some people with whom I've shared these tips think, "I don't have time to spend 8-12 hours mapping out all of the little details that come up! That's a waste of time!" Actually, it is a "waste of time" *not* to create systems. Why? Because the next time you need to prepare for the same task or event, you'll be doubling the hours you spend working on it unnecessarily. A dedication to creating systems means that you will shave off hours in the future. That 12 hours of investment, over time, is going to pay out in massive time dividends. Systems take time, but systems also make time.

The secret to automation is creating systems.

Over the years, people have been blown away at how many balls I've had in my court. I began to be referred to in our church as "the systems guy." I'd create a series of repeatable processes that others could effectively pull off without my direct involvement. I would work diligently with those individuals on the front end to ensure that I was not missing anything.

Over time, when we put systems in place and had the right people doing the right things, the system fed itself and provided extra time to everyone involved. You may not be the type of person who finds thinking ahead easy. If you don't have the spiritual gift of administration, find someone who does. You'd be surprised how much automation can be implemented in your ministry—and it's all through systems. Systems take time, and systems make time.

TAKEAWAY

In your own words, how are systems different from automation in general? Why do you need systems in order to automate processes in your ministry?

_____

_____

_____

_____

_____

_____

_____

_____

_____

_____

_____

_____

_____

_____

_____

_____

_____

_____

19

THE TRAP OF THE CLEAN STALL

You've likely heard that old saying, "If you want a job done right, do it yourself!" This is, many times, the attitude we adopt in our ministries. We do our best to avoid messes, mistakes, and the "human" element of operating a ministry; in the end, though, this causes us to step into "The Trap of the Clean Stall."

Proverbs 14:4 reads, "Where there are no oxen, the manger is clean, but much increase comes by the strength of the ox." In the ancient agrarian world, animals brought a massive advantage. To have an animal meant you had power: power to increase the harvest and get the job done. The writer of Proverbs says that it is really a trade-off. On one hand, you got a significant increase through the strength of your ox; yet with the ox comes ox-sized messes. Namely, ox poop.

Let's compare the alternative: you have no oxen, and you have an amazingly clean manger stall. The decision is whether or not you want more harvest with a poopy stall vs. a perfectly clean stall with a diminished harvest.

Our goal is not a clean stall. Our goal is a huge harvest. A natural side effect of huge harvests is messes. A tidy stall in and of itself is a bad trade for a compromised harvest. Remember, I have a well-managed case of OCD. I crave order. I hate disorder. Yet the calling of the harvest trumps our desire for order. Do not fall into the trap of the clean stall.

A tidy stall in and of itself is a bad trade for a compromised harvest.

We must define and redefine our harvest goal: reaching the lost through equipping the fold. Our ultimate goal is not order for order's sake. Our goal is the good news of Jesus going deep into the hearts and heads of those we serve. This brings mess. Get used to it, and get over it.

Let's take this proverbial analogy a step further. You, as a ministry leader, are essentially the farmer. You can't and don't want to your work alone—you need help. Those willing to help you from staff or volunteer positions bring great strength—together, you accomplish more for the harvest than you do by yourself.

Both oxen and people bring messes. Farming is messy. Jesus said He came not for the healthy but for the sick. Sick people have issues and need attention. That is our job. Years ago, someone sarcastically said, "Ministry would be great were it not for all these *people!*" The harvest is plentiful, but the workers are few. More workers equals more mess. We as farmers must manage the mess and rise above looking at the stall to see the harvest. Do you want a harvest more than you want order? Absolutely. Therefore, we have to embrace the reality of a poopy stall. Do not fall into the trap of the clean stall.

TAKEAWAY

What are a few ways that Jesus displayed a willingness to get his hands dirty during His earthly ministry? How did he link arms with others in His efforts to reach the lost? What can you change in your ministry to begin embracing mess and letting go of the fantasy of a "clean stall"?

_____

_____

_____

_____

_____

_____

20

SWITCHING, NOT DITCHING

Your phone rings with the dreaded Saturday night phone call. Even as you answer i6, you know how this conversation will go: one of your volunteers is canceling. That inevitable phone call, text, email says "I'm sorry, I can't come in tomorrow because..." followed by the rationale for why a volunteer can't fulfill the commitment they've made.

The more volunteers that serve in your ministry, the greater the likelihood is that someone will cancel this weekend, leaving you scrambling at the last minute for a substitute. I understand this frustration all too well. Over time, however, I figured out a way not be a part of that last-minute scramble. I wanted to create a culture of switching, not ditching. We wanted to place the burden on the *volunteer* to find their own substitute, so we created a system that allowed individuals to call their teammates and ask if they could swap weeks with them.

Now, before you cry "foul" and say that you've tried this before and it's a woeful failure, there are a couple of ground rules that must be established before you implement this strategy:

You need to have a fantastic relationship with all of your volunteers. They cannot see this strategy as a burden. You want them to view it as a wonderful service. We created a culture allowing people to see their fellow teammates as willing participants in carrying out the goals of the ministry: a culture of switching, not ditching.

We created a culture allowing people to see their fellow teammates as willing participants in carrying out the goals of the ministry.

Find out the best means of contact for each team member. Do you serve in the preschool ministry? Great! Twelve other people may fit that qualification. Of those twelve people, three would most likely be reached by phone. The others might be best reached through a text message. These individuals have a relationship with one another and know these things, because we as leaders created a culture of relationship.

Here's the bottom line: my life is made easier when volunteers work out some details on their own. Our volunteers are more than willing to solve scheduling conflicts, because they have relationships with staff and other volunteers. When people aren't anonymous in your ministry, they understand that their teammates have lives, just like they do. They know that, at some point, they are going to need the favor returned.

Do you want to avoid the painful and problematic last-minute calls informing you that somebody isn't coming? Create a culture of switching, not ditching.

TAKEAWAY

How strong are the bonds between your volunteers? Do you think they would feel comfortable asking one another to cover their shifts? If not, what are a few ways you can foster better relationships between them. If so, what have you done to create these relationships to date?

_____

_____

_____

_____

_____

_____

_____

_____

_____

21

PROMISE LITTLE, PRODUCE MUCH

All ministry leaders desire to please the people we shepherd. Part of this involves letting our people know what we plan to do—our future vision, and the ideas we have for improving the ministry. As ideas and visions are shared, people begin to identify with what you bring to the table, and consider your ideas as promises to be fulfilled.

But what happens when the ideas and visions you share are not brought to fruition? The people who heard your promises will be woefully disappointed. An important leadership principal for all ministry leaders is to under-promise and over-deliver. This may sound like common sense but, as many of us have experienced, common sense is often *not* so common.

Certainly, we want to share upcoming ideas and future visions with those we lead. Just as Jesus shared in the gospels, however, we need to count the cost before seeking to build the tower: Luke 14:28-30 says, "'For which of you, desiring to build a tower, does not first sit down and count the cost, whether he has enough to complete it? Otherwise, when he has laid a foundation and is not able to finish, all who see it begin to mock him, saying, 'This man began to build and was not able to finish.'" While this verse is originally talking about counting the cost of following Christ, it can also be applied to our endeavors in ministry.

The last thing we want to do is to gain a reputation for being all talk and no game.

Many leaders have shot themselves in the foot by communicating a grand vision but not following through to bring it to fruition. Let's imagine that you have a vision, and the completion of that vision is represented by the number 10. It would be better for you to say nothing and achieve a 4 than to sell the idea of a 10 but only produce a 4.

Watch what you share with people before its time. Say less and produce a lot. People want to see results; they don't want to hear empty words and promises. The last thing we want to do is to gain a reputation for being all talk and no game. Promise little, but produce much.

TAKEAWAY

What are three vision items that you feel comfortable sharing with the people you lead, because you can pretty much ensure that they're going to happen? What are three vision items that you need to keep close to your chest right now, because they're still in the planning stages?

_____

_____

_____

_____

_____

_____

_____

_____

_____

_____

_____

_____

_____

_____

_____

22

MEASURE TWICE, CUT ONCE

Over the years, I've become friends with many carpenters. For some reason, God has placed many individuals from the construction industry into my life. I've spent time with them, and sought to learn their trade—to no avail. I'm just not a handy guy. Regardless, I learned a very important principle that my construction friends work by: measure twice, cut once.

Sometimes, I'd be working with my friend, The Finnish Carpenter. This man had expensive wood that he would use to make crown molding and beautiful Finnish carpentry sculptures inside million-dollar homes. Sometimes, he actually allowed me to make some cuts and help him. I don't know why he did this, but I picked up some valuable lessons from him. With the expensive wood he used, we only had one shot. If I cut a piece of expensive oak in the wrong place, the entire board would be rendered useless—not an effective strategy.

**Being an intelligent leader involves acting
with discipline and diligence.**

Ministry leaders need to think about our changes, communications, and even our emails. Think about them twice, and then pull the trigger once. If I take an extra three to four minutes to reread my email prior to sending it, that's measuring twice and cutting once. Once I hit *Send*, I can't retract those words. Before making a change in ministry, I go through a series of checks and balances, questions, and double-checking before I communicate the change.

Let's say I have a challenging parent meeting coming up with a parent who's upset. I don't necessarily know yet how I'm going to handle the situation. I only get one shot to be face-to-face with this parent. If I fail to plan, I could end up reopening this issue four or five times just to get my phrasing right; or I could spend the time making sure that I script out my words and craft them carefully. I may not use that script during the meeting, but it allows me to gather my thoughts on paper ahead of time. That's measuring twice.

Being an intelligent leader involves acting with discipline and diligence—it's being thoughtful instead of impulsive. An impulsive carpenter wastes a lot of wood. An impulsive ministry leader burns a lot of bridges. Measure twice, cut once.

TAKEAWAY

Can you think of any initiatives, meetings, or plans that are on your horizon right now that provide an opportunity for you to measure twice, cut once? Practically, what does that preparation look like in each of the scenarios you listed?

_____

_____

_____

_____

_____

_____

_____

_____

_____

_____

_____

_____

_____

_____

_____

23

QUIETLY ALLOW RESULTS TO SPEAK FOR THEMSELVES

Years ago, our team decided to undertake a massive endeavor—we recreated and redesigned all of our brochures. This may seem like a simple task, but it wasn't. We started from scratch. It took us a little over a year to effectively craft what we felt was the perfect set of brochures and handouts. We worked with a graphic designer, labored hard to wordsmith our copy, got valuable feedback, and made modifications. When the palette of brochures was finally published, we printed them on high-quality, expensive material. I must say, we were quite proud of our brochures.

Time moved on, and the brochures had been handed out for a while. One day, at a staff meeting, I could tell that our senior pastor was somewhat off. He came in with a characteristic pained look, and used the entire staff meeting to systematically lay out all the brochures and paraphernalia that we had promoting items and events at our church. I saw our set of brochures among the many, and wondered what he might say.

In time, our quiet excellence was noticed and rewarded.

As he went through each piece of literature, he criticized and critiqued — noting if it was subpar, unclear, or inconsistent with what he wanted. This took about an hour. At the end, he came to two sets of brochures—the one our team had created, and one that had been created based off of ours.

He held up our brochures, and I swallowed hard. The pastor opened his mouth, and said, "Moving forward, every piece of literature that comes from this church must follow this pattern. This is the new standard at our church."

I was blown away. We had worked so hard for over a year to diligently craft what we hoped would be the perfect set of brochures. After that year, we waited another year-and-a-half before receiving any acknowledgement or accolade from the staff. Another department had tried to replicate what we had done; but overall, our efforts had gone almost completely unnoticed.

However, at just the right time, our efforts and labors were recognized. We desired that our excellence speak for itself. We didn't stand up at the staff meeting and decry the atrocities of every other ministry's brochures. It wasn't our place. Our place was to do an excellent job with what we had responsibility over. In time, our quiet excellence was noticed and rewarded.

This is my encouragement to you: quietly allow your results to speak for themselves.

TAKEAWAY

Can you recall a time that someone *else* was the first to point out something excellent about your ministry? Did this make you feel differently compared when *you're* the one pointing out your own successes? What did this experience teach you?

_____

_____

_____

_____

_____

_____

_____

_____

_____

_____

24

OVERWHELM WITH EXCELLENCE

I think an important value we need to subscribe to in ministry is excellence. For far too long, I have seen quality take a back seat to expediency. "Getting it done" has eclipsed getting it done *well*. Over the years, this attitude has been a sad stain on so many ministries, whose activities and programs are pulled off in a subpar fashion.

We've all heard ministry leaders say things like, "Well, we're doing it for the Lord, not for human glory." They somehow use this as an excuse for their average performance...which seems counterintuitive to me. If we *are* doing this for the Lord, shouldn't we do it with even *more* excellence?

My question to most ministry leaders is, "Would you submit this work at a Fortune 500 company? I doubt it." Now, some of you may push back and reply, "We don't have the resources that a Fortune 500 company has; we can only do ministry with the resources we have."

For far too long, I have seen quality take a back seat to expediency.

I agree. However, there is a difference between an excellence mentality and a "this is good enough for the church" mentality. Over the years, I've watched Christianity create a reputation for having subpar, C-level work. Somehow, we think that since it's for the Lord, He understands. Instead, the knowledge that He is watching over everything we do in His name should cause a *greater* level of intentionality and excellence in the work we do.

I cringe at messy ministry areas, half-baked brochures, and training meetings that are just plain pathetic. Business leaders who choose to volunteer in the church shouldn't be ashamed of our work, or of partnering with us. I personally want to do better. Whenever anyone interacts with a ministry I'm involved with, I want to overwhelm them with excellence. Whether it's a PowerPoint, a piece of literature, a video, or an email, I want to take extra time and intentionality to make it shine.

Overwhelm with excellence. Do things with a quality that is worthy of the name of Christ.

TAKEAWAY

Why do you think the church has adopted, in large part, a mentality of "This is *good enough?*" Can you think of any other practices in the church or in our society that reinforce this tendency to settle for C-level service?

_____

_____

_____

_____

_____

_____

_____

_____

_____

_____

_____

_____

_____

_____

_____

_____

25

HE WHO CHASES TWO
RABBITS CATCHES NONE

I've seen so many ministry leaders be far less effective because they chase many rabbits at once. In my backyard, I have plenty of rabbits. I don't like them, but it's fun when my young children chase them around. As you well know, they never catch the rabbit. A rabbit is fast—it can turn on a dime and quickly find safety hiding under a bush or rock.

Now, think about how much more difficult it would be to catch two rabbits! They each could go in different directions, leaving you standing in the middle, staring foolishly at nothing. He who chases two rabbits catches none. If you diligently work to chase one rabbit, you might be able to cut the corner and catch it in your clutches. But catching two rabbits is an impossibility.

So many ministry leaders have tried to tackle six or seven brand new goals at the same time. Every one of those agendas requires their attention, their effort, and their hours. When we seek to tackle too much at once, we actually fail at everything. I'm a firm believer in choosing a rabbit and chasing it down until that crazy thing is caught.

**When we seek to tackle too much at once,
we actually fail at everything.**

If I'm going to tackle a new ministry initiative, I'm going to focus almost exclusively on that initiative. I'm not going to try to work on three or four at once. Each one has enough work of its own. I'm going to focus on one thing, execute, and ensure that the rabbit is not only caught but cleaned, cooked, and eaten.

Our eyes (and minds and hearts) often are far bigger than our abilities. Our dreams often surpass our ability to execute. Whether we're looking at in business, ministry, or our own personal lives, we would do far better to prioritize what we *really* want to do and simply focus on doing that one thing. It may take three months, six months, or even a year; but if you dedicate yourself to one thing and truly seek to knock it out of the park, you're more likely to do so. When we're honest, the six-or-seven-rabbits-at-once approach simply doesn't bring meaningful results.

Stick with one rabbit. He who chases two rabbits catches none. Be wise, pick a rabbit, and chase that thing until you've got it in your clutches.

TAKEAWAY

Why is it so tempting to try chasing more than one "rabbit" at once? Have you tried (or are you currently trying) to chase two or more initiatives at the same time? How does this affect the level of excellence you're able to bring to each initiative? Lastly, identify one thing that's most important to you in business, ministry, or your personal life—what "rabbit" do you want to absolutely commit to chasing right now?

_____

_____

_____

_____

_____

_____

_____

_____

_____

_____

26

DON'T RECRUIT DISUNIFYING PEOPLE

I made a significant mistake early on in my ministry career. It wasn't making unpopular decisions—after all, we'll all make calls that won't please everyone... that just comes with the territory. My mistake, however, was recruiting individuals who were vehemently and publically opposed to the changes I was making.

My mistake was the result of the old axiom, "Keep your friends close and your enemies closer." Of course, I don't want to view these individuals as my enemies by any stretch of the imagination. However, I thought this principle could apply to bringing people close that were opposed to me, so I could keep a close eye on them or seek to win them over. Deep down, at a heart level, I assumed that my powers of persuasion and relational savvy could make them see that my methods were worthwhile. I thought, naively, that having them participate in the ministry would bring them to "my side."

This couldn't have been further from the truth. Instead, I recruited publicly disunifying figures. I brought them close to the sheep. I brought them close to other volunteers. I made a mistake that hurt everyone in my ministry.

**If they are disunifying, keep them away
from the sheep. Don't recruit them.**

What were the results of that mistake? Every Monday morning, I saw an email come in from one disunifying volunteer in particular. About the length of a book, it was filled with fault-finding, nitpicking, and criticism of nearly everything we were doing as a ministry. It was crafted in such a way that it truly necessitated a response. This interaction sucked energy from me every week—energy that was already in short supply.

This individual refused to see the positives in the ministry, because their heart was out of joint. Nothing I did would change that. In the end, it was a connection that sowed disunity and frustration within the ministry, without any payoff or increased mutual understanding.

Here's the deal: the last thing you we want to do is to take someone who is disunifying and elevate them to a higher level of authority or influence within your ministry. If they are disunifying, keep them away from the sheep. Don't recruit them. This individual had been placed in a position of prominence as a small group leader. Other church members could go to this person and ask them about their perspective of the ministry. It would be best, of course, for someone to come directly to me and ask me a question, but guess what? That typically doesn't happen.

So, when you recruit disunifying people who have relationships within the church, and other people come to them instead of you, they are going to get an earful of why things are so bad. You are now providing an opportunity for this cancer to spread. That's a bold term—but I want you to know that recruiting and elevating disunifying individuals is quite possibly one of the most dangerous moves you could make as a leader in ministry.

Do not recruit disunifying people. Do not let them near the sheep. Exercise wisdom in who you recruit and who you promote in your ministry.

TAKEAWAY

What are some of the warning signs you've seen in volunteers that indicate a disunifying spirit? Have you ever had to handle a situation with a disunifying volunteer before? What was the result? What did you learn from this experience?

_____

_____

_____

_____

LEADERSHIP DEVELOPMENT

27

ATTENDING YOUR OWN MINISTRY EVENT

This idea sounds like common logic. Who in their right mind would plan an event but not attend it themselves?

Ministry is so complex; there are times in which so much is going on that you are tempted not to be fully present—even for events you've poured hours into planning. I served at a rather large church. In order to survive, I had to be very adept at delegation. After all, in ministry, if you don't delegate, you're going to die. You have to create a team around you to pull off all of the various events and ministries under your watch.

In the process of delegating, I built a team. I poured into them relationally and experientially, giving them all the tools they needed. I built such effective systems that I could have chosen not to be present at our events, because I knew everything would go smoothly.

My absence will be noticed far more than my presence.

Now, I have to push pause and say this: there once was a leader I watched who felt that great leadership was working himself out of a job. At face value, I agree. However, for a number of years, I watched this leader direct one of his church's largest events: he showed up late, stood around, and then left early before all of the tasks were finished.

The individuals who had responsibilities delegated to them began to feel resentment towards the leader. Why? It's simple—many people think that my job consists of nothing but Sunday morning. You and I know that there is so much more to ministry than a time block of a few hours. The challenge is this: since they don't know what we do, when we don't show up at an event, people wonder, "Why are we paying him? What does he even do?"

It's a tricky balance. Even if I have delegated, I need to be a leader who is present—from the very beginning until the last chair is put up and the last piece of popcorn is vacuumed. My role may be to encourage, inspire, and pat people on the back; but my absence will be noticed far more than my presence.

Every one of the individuals to whom I have delegated have a 40-hour a week job; they have families; they have obligations—a yard to mow and dinner to cook. I need to understand that they are sacrificing to be a part of a team. If their leader is missing-in-action, and feels too busy to be a part of the event, he or she has insulted and failed them. People will feel resentful—angry—they will see you as less than a leader. Don't get me wrong—you *can* find reprieve as a ministry leader — just not by missing your own events.

At the end of the day, be present at your own ministry events.

TAKEAWAY

Why do you think it's tempting for ministry leaders to skip out on attending certain events or occasions? What other forms of reprieve can you find that are healthier for both you and your team?

_____

_____

_____

_____

_____

_____

_____

28

CHILL OUT – IT USUALLY WORKS OUT

I've been in ministry for a long time. Early on, when our nursery director texted or called to tell me that four people called in sick at 7:00 p.m. on Saturday night, I would freak out! The thoughts would start racing through my head: *We're going to be shorthanded. The quality of our ministry won't be as high. Will our ratios be acceptable? What if more people call in tomorrow morning?*

Eventually, I realized I had two choices when this happened. I can freak out and lose sleep scurrying to find people, *or* I can understand that I've done my part. Our team sought to develop a healthy substitute list, and we will do our part to make it work. However, at the end of the day, we are going to let it go and trust God to take care of His church.

This is a lesson I learned from our nursery directors, two dear women who served faithfully for many years. God taught them some valuable lessons that they passed on to me. Our experiences together included a time when, on a Sunday morning, there was a massive snow storm; the exact number of people who cancelled fit perfectly with the number of kids who didn't show up because of the storm. From experiences like this, I learned to hang on and chill out. It usually works out and comes together. *Time and time again, we have watched God provide.*

When your volunteers are falling off the grid,
understand that God has things under control.

In another experience, we were short-handed and on a Sunday and three youth workers— the best that we have — said, "We need to fulfill school service hours, and this is the only weekend we can do it. Can we step in?" God takes care of His church.

Over time, I began to develop this muscle of faith. That doesn't mean I'm going to sleep at the wheel and not do my part. I still need to develop a rigorous, healthy bench of players and have a strong substitute list. However, I have learned to "let go and let God."

We trusted God and did our part. Then, we relinquished control. Time and time again, God came through for us. He has an amazing way of just making things happen. So, when your volunteers are falling off the grid, understand that God has things under control. Chill out. Things usually work out.

TAKEAWAY

Can you recall a time that God came in at a desperate moment in your ministry and met a need? What did this experience teach you? What are some dire needs that you have right now? Write a short prayer surrendering control to God, and expressing faith in Him to continually meet your needs.

_____

_____

_____

_____

_____

_____

_____

_____

_____

_____

_____

_____

_____

29

CONCERNED ABOUT MANY THINGS

I may be concerned about many things, but I am only responsible but for a few. I've learned to direct my energies towards the few. Over the years, I have seen illogical, poor decision-making on the part of ministries in my church—ministries in which I had no responsibility. Let me give you an example of this.

Let's imagine that there is a ministry adjacent to me. The leader of this ministry is my peer. I do not oversee them, and they do not oversee me. However, I've observed a new idea they are trying to tackle. This idea doesn't make sense to me, and it's being executed poorly. *Wait!* Why is this *my* problem? Yet, on more than one occasion, I've gotten my underwear into a wad about other people's problems. I've experienced anxiety and fretful evenings simply because of someone else's lack of execution, or poor execution.

Of course, I want everything to go well in the church. However, I don't have responsibility over everything in the church. I only have responsibility for a few things. I can acknowledge when I am concerned about something while still remembering that I'm not responsible for that thing. To be concerned about another ministry area doing a poor job is understandable—it reflects poorly on us as a church. However, draw the line. Express your concern, acknowledge your emotions, and then turn your attention to the areas that *you* have responsibility over.

I don't have responsibility over everything in the church. I only have responsibility for a few things.

Do you know what *you* are responsible for? You've been entrusted with certain aspects of ministry. You are responsible to your supervisor and, ultimately, to the Lord, in these areas. Take those areas the most seriously. When you unnecessarily focus on areas that are not your responsibility, you're wasting precious time and energy. When I identify that another area of ministry is doing something I think could be done differently, I have found success by turning my attention to the areas for which I have responsibility—simply making sure that my area does not make that same mistake.

I had a leader years ago who conducted some of the worst meetings I'd ever been a part of. Unfortunately, as I sat in these meetings, I became frustrated, upset, angry, and anxious about what a colossal waste of time they were. Not only was I wasting emotional energy, but I wasn't doing my heart any good by getting frustrated at this leader. This leader was my superior, so I had no hope of actually changing the way that these meetings were conducted.

Instead, I decided to zero in on the things that were frustrating me, and then apply those insights to the way I conducted meetings. Lo and behold, I discovered that my own meetings also had some gaping oversights. Why was I complaining about someone else's meetings when I had deficiencies in my own leadership? This experience changed my entire perspective on fault-finding and personal responsibility.

Before you complain about someone else's ministry, make sure that your area of ministry is not falling into the same traps. I am concerned about many things, but I am responsible but for a few. Focus on *your* few.

TAKEAWAY

Below, list out what your "few" responsibilities encompass. What falls under your purview? Now, think about the things you've been frustrated or anxious about in the last few weeks. Are any of these responsibilities *not* yours? If so, which ones?

_____

_____

_____

_____

30

WHEN YOU SUCCEED, LOOK OUT THE WINDOW

Healthy leaders understand who has helped them, who has supported them, and who got them to the victory that they are reveling in today. I seek to create teams—to build people and create processes. Interestingly enough, when I have a victory, it's never one that I've won on my own. Only a fool would think such a thing. Our victories in ministry have dozens of people behind them. Ministry is not a solo event—it's a team sport.

Think for a moment about the actress who stands up at an award ceremony after being handed a gold statue. Although it's somewhat annoying to the rest of us, she goes on for as long as they let her, thanking everyone who was involved in making this opportunity a reality for her. The actress wins the award, but there are hundreds of people who do their part in order to make that happen. In the same way, if you sit in a position of leadership, don't be fooled into thinking that your victories have been achieved exclusively by your own efforts. It's simply not true. Teams win victories.

Ministry is not a solo event—it's a team sport.

When you win, look out the window and celebrate the contributions of all. Conversely, when you fail, look in the mirror. Now, that's a hard one—it's super easy to point an accusing finger at our teams when we fail. But what good is that going to do you? Instead, what if you were to look in the mirror and ask yourself what about your leadership caused them not to be able to do their job? Did they not have the resources that they needed? Did they not have adequate instructions from you? Did they not have an adequate picture of the vision from you? Typically, when things haven't gone well, and I look in the mirror, it becomes obvious where I've failed my team—usually, it's because of my lack of involvement.

When it doesn't go well, look in the mirror. Could you have been more clear in your instructions? Could you have spent more time articulating the vision to a time-strapped volunteer? Could you have created a more realistic timeline? At the end of the day, when it doesn't go well, where should the blame fall? Honestly, it should fall on the leader. If I am honest, humble, and transparent, I have tremendous opportunity for self-reflection and growth.

When a victory happens, look out the window at the team who supported you. When a failure happens, look in the mirror and assess how you could have lead differently.

TAKEAWAY

Think of a recent victory you've had—how did your team contribute to achieving it? Think of a recent failure you've had—how did your own leadership contribute to it?

_____

_____

_____

_____

_____

_____

_____

_____

_____

_____

_____

_____

_____

31

DON'T GIVE AWAY THE KEYS

Let's imagine for a moment that you're at an off-site event with a group of kids and volunteers. You stop at a gas station, and are filling up your fifteen-passenger van when an individual you've never met before walks up to you. He boldly thrusts out his hand, shakes yours vigorously, and says, "My name is Bill. Will you give me the keys to that van?"

You have been entrusted with the lives of the kids in this van by their parents. If you're in your right mind, there's no way you'd surrender the keys to this stranger. Now, imagine that this individual begins to get pushy. "Listen," he says, "I don't know why you're hesitating. Look at my driver's license. I have been a fantastic driver all my life. Give me the keys to the van."

Avert massive leadership disaster by insisting on a season of "getting to know you."

Though this sounds like a comical situation, this has happened to me in ministry on more than one occasion. Individuals with a firm agenda sought me out, resume in hand, to tell me what they think we should do with our ministry. Individuals new to the church will abruptly introduce themselves and begin sharing the wonderful things they did at their last church. They're eager to get involved and have experience to bring to the table. At first glance, this might seem like a wonderful thing. Sometimes, though, these individuals introduce themselves in a less-than-appropriate, assertive fashion. They want to implement their program and their agenda into your ministry. They've just met you—they don't understand your culture, and yet they're asking for the keys to the car.

We are all in need of volunteers. You don't, however, want to intersect and engage with someone who is demanding the keys this early in the game. If the first time you meet someone they are pushy, forward, and off-putting, you can only expect more of the same. Trust me, I speak from experience.

Put into place some simple boundaries and barriers. Avert massive leadership disaster by insisting on a season of "getting to know you." Say to this individual, "We're so excited for this opportunity. We'd love for you to get to know us, and to get to know you. The culture we've created is one in which you serve you for the first six months; as you learn the rhythm of our ministry over time, we'll find out where you fit and really make the highest contribution."

Interestingly enough, on both occasions where I had an individual try to aggressively assert their agenda, they left almost instantly. Their actions said, "If I can't have it my way, I won't have it any way." Disaster was averted because we'd set boundaries in place. You've been given the charge of caring for and nurturing this ministry. Give people time to get acclimated to your church before inserting themselves. Don't give away the keys to the car.

TAKEAWAY

What's your current strategy for onboarding eager volunteers? What about communicating with and placing aggressive volunteers? Is there anything you feel you need to strengthen about your strategies in these areas?

32

DOES YOUR STRATEGY CLARIFY OPPORTUNITIES?

Ministry leaders can easily fall prey to shiny, silver objects. It's all too easy to be derailed from a critical strategy by a shiny object that's appeared in your periphery. When you begin to pursue these kinds of peripheral opportunities, you quickly get off track.

Think of your strategy as a die cast mold, set beforehand, that determines your future outcomes. To make a die cast mold, liquid metal is poured into a predetermined shape. The metal, once cooled, takes on the form of the mold. For your ministry strategy to be like a die cast mold, you must predetermine where you want to go and what you want your outcome to look like. Far too many leaders have no strategy—every random, seemingly positive opportunity automatically redefines where they're going. These leaders jerk the proverbial wheel right to left, left to right, causing their passengers to get seasick.

One of the most important leadership characteristics you can have is the ability to create a strategy and literally stick with it. Be immovable. Seek the Lord. Seek counsel. Strategically determine where you want to go in the next few years. Be disciplined and committed to that opportunity.

Far too many leaders have no strategy—every random, seemingly positive opportunity automatically redefines where they're going.

Commitment doesn't mean you're rigid, or that you resist any future opportunities. It simply means that you have a bias toward the word, "No." There are far too many opportunities that will derail and dismantle a wonderful future. Learn to say no.

A great leader once said, "A wonderful *yes* can predetermine the next one thousand *nos.*" In other words, having a critical, prayer-based strategy automatically redirects you from the opportunities that are of lesser quality in your life. Having a bias towards "No" allows you to say your greatest "Yes."

Does your strategy help you quickly determine "Yes" or "No"? Or is your strategy so undefined—or even nonexistent—that any opportunity is open game? Without a strong strategy, we'll find ourselves achieving nothing at all. At the end of the day, make a winning strategy and stick to it. Don't be tempted by every random, shiny object in your field of vision.

TAKEAWAY

What are the select few priorities, opportunities, and actions you've committed to say "Yes" to? What are some of the things you've decided to say "No" to in order to pursue your strategy?

_____

_____

_____

_____

_____

_____

_____

_____

_____

_____

_____

_____

_____

33

DON'T CRY WOLF

Full disclosure: I'm someone who can easily succumb to using exaggeration, hyperbole, and dramatic inflation. I have to be careful not to exaggerate the needs of our ministry to others in order to get our way. You probably know what I'm talking about: you sit in front of your supervisor and say you want one of three things: an increase in budget, an increase in space, or an increase in volunteers. Only...you stretch the truth just a little bit.

You want an increased budget, so you paint a picture of your ministry as it stands with its current budget. You need more volunteers, so you explain to your supervisor about all the volunteers you don't currently have, and the desperate needs that you do have. You may explain how cramped your space is, and how the need for just one or two more rooms is of utmost importance.

I've been a children's pastor for over a decade; I know that these are not only common problems, but they will continue to be problems within all of our ministries. Money is a limited. Volunteers are a hot commodity. Square footage in your church is typically a limited commodity (and it's rare that your church will agree to blow out two walls and add another 10,000 square feet of space).

Don't find yourself characterized as an exaggerated tale-spinner of half-truths in order to get your way.

Limited resources can feel as if they're limiting your ministry. I get it. However, you *will* be hurt if you exaggerate your ministry needs and your supervisor does due diligence to explore whether or not your story holds water. I have found myself in front of my executive pastor, over-exaggerating the needs of my ministry in order to get them placed at the top of the pile of things he needs to do.

Stretching the truth might work the first few times, but it's a pathetic long-term strategy. Soon, you're going to be caught crying wolf. You know the story—the young shepherd cries wolf, the townspeople come running, and there is not a wolf at all. Fool me once, your fault; fool me twice, my fault. The second and third times he cries wolf, the townspeople not only think skeptically about coming—the third time, they don't come at all. They see the shepherd's need as extremely suspect, and possibly even an outright lie. You do *not* want to be in this position. Don't exaggerate the needs of your ministry. Don't find yourself characterized as an exaggerated tale-spinner of half-truths in order to get your way. Trust me, it won't pay off.

TAKEAWAY

Write out a legitimate need that you have in your ministry right now. Then, below it, write an "exaggerated" version—something you could share with your supervisor that wouldn't be a completely accurate representation of your need. What differences in tone, attitude, and scope do you see between the two?

_____

_____

_____

_____

_____

_____

_____

_____

_____

_____

_____

_____

34

EAT THAT FROG

A number of years ago, while sitting in an airport, I saw an interesting book with a familiar title: *Eat That Frog* by Brian Tracey, a well-known productivity guru. Let's imagine you sit down to dinner with your 5-year-old, and he or she looks at the plate and sees broccoli, steaming mac and cheese, and fresh raspberries. In their mind, they're so eager to eat the mac and cheese, and those bright red raspberries, but they know the broccoli is *not* something that they want to partake of.

There are two strategies for your child at this point. They can eat the hardest thing first and get it down—then the rest of the plate is quite a joy to consume. Or they can eat everything they like first, and then be left with that horrible, bitter-tasting broccoli.

Brian Tracy suggests that we tackle the hardest, most intense, most demanding tasks first. He advises leaders to dedicate an hour or two in the beginning of the day to the most audacious things—the things we're most likely to put off. Do those first. With the remainder of your day, you can easily crank out benign emails, brainless tasks, and clean your plate. Instead, what happens to many leaders, myself included, is that we jump in, spend the best part of our brainpower and energy combing through low-grade, low-importance tasks, and then have nothing left for the important, gargantuan task at the end of the day.

**Do the hardest thing first, and the rest of your
small tasks can be done quickly.**

Do I want to try to tackle that big, fat, ugly frog at 3:42 p.m., knowing I'm not going to make it very far?

Brian Tracey's book has been revolutionary for me. If I can dedicate the first hours of my day toward the most critical tasks, I find myself moving important things forward. At the end of the day, there is always time to crank through small emails and checklists. Those things can happen pretty quickly. In addition, when we have a time constraint, we often allow those tasks to fill up the time we have allotted to it. As an example, if I give an hour of my time to email, I could spend two hours tinkering around, trying to solve low-level problems. However, if I have 30 minutes before the day is over and I have a list of emails to go through, I find myself to be extraordinarily efficient.

Do the hardest thing first, and the rest of your small tasks can be done quickly. Eat that frog!

TAKEAWAY

Think about your daily routine. What usually takes up the first 1-2 hours of your day—when science says we're most alert and effective? When do you usually end up tackling big, important projects? What do you want to change about your current daily routine?

_____

_____

_____

_____

_____

_____

_____

_____

_____

_____

_____

35

FEEL FREE TO SAY NO

In ministry, I want to make sure that my personal powers of persuasion are not leveraged as manipulation. People need to listen to the voice of the Holy Spirit, not my voice. I don't want to convince someone, in a pressured situation, that they should be volunteering—that's not my job.

I understand—we all need volunteers. However, you don't want the *wrong* volunteers. You don't want someone to respond to *your* persuasion rather than the power of the Holy Spirit. I've overtly encouraged people to pray about their decision—if they don't feel God leading them to serve, then I tell them, "By all means, please say no." It would be a train wreck for them—and for you! —if they agreed to volunteer but didn't feel that God was truly calling them.

You don't want someone to respond to *your* persuasion rather than the power of the Holy Spirit.

Don't forget: you hold some form of authority in the life of your church. Be cautious. Don't seek to leverage that authority in an inappropriate way. You are not the junior Holy Spirit. As leaders, we can allocate our gifts and abilities in such a way that compels people to act in certain ways—depending on how we use this power, it can be very dangerous.

People need to be compelled to volunteer by Lord Almighty. How much more powerful will they be if God, not you, has called them? I don't want to be a manipulative leader. I want to be a leader who leads people to see, hear, and respond to the voice of the Holy Spirit. Would you rather have people say "no" to you honestly, or feel guilt, pressure, and persuasion to say "yes" insincerely? Please, do everyone a favor—give them the freedom to say no.

TAKEAWAY

How do you leave room in your recruiting approach for people to say "no"?

_____

_____

_____

_____

_____

_____

_____

_____

_____

_____

_____

_____

_____

_____

_____

_____

_____

_____

_____

_____

_____

_____

_____

_____

36

END YOUR DAY WITH TOMORROW

In my ministry growth and development, I stumbled upon a fantastic strategy. It not only works for me, but is also in keeping with verified brain research. The brain is an interesting organ—it's constantly seeking to solve problems and tasks. Have you ever had a moment when you're trying to remember something, it's on the tip of your tongue, and then several minutes later it pops into your head? When you can't remember something, your mind starts combing through files in your short- and long-term memory. It goes on a search-and-locate mission. Even when your conscious mind can't grasp onto the fact, your subconscious mind is still very active. Maybe 10 or 12 minutes later, you have what's called an "out-of-the-blue moment." *BING!* Your mind wouldn't rest until it found that piece of information.

Your brain is always at work on a subconscious level. Why not activate your brain to work for you even while you sleep?

The same thing happens when we try to solve a problem or complete a task: your mind seeks to find the most efficient way to solve the problem. If I wake up and create my to-do list first thing in the morning, my mind begins trying to solve the problems in the list. However, if I start the night before by writing that same list, my brain starts to subconsciously solve those very problems in the most efficient way possible, literally as I sleep.

Before you go to bed, if you engage your subconscious in regards to what you're planning to do the next morning, your efficiency improves. You save time. On a more fundamental level, your brain has already been engaged for the past 7-9 hours in preparation to solve your problems—it's ready to tackle complex challenges as soon as you roll out of bed! Your brain is always at work on a subconscious level. Why not activate your brain to work for you even while you sleep?

Some of you may say, "I can't do that—I'm going to write my task list, and then I'll lie in bed all night thinking about those things!" That is your conscious mind. I understand that this may be a pitfall for some. However, you can overcome that problem. Over time, you can train your mind to turn off.

Let's say you "download" your to-dos out of your brain and onto paper; then, you have an evening routine that helps your conscious mind to say, "Those are tasks for tomorrow. I am relinquishing responsibility out of my conscious mind." When you put routines and rhythms like this into place, eventually, your subconscious mind will kick in and take over.

My encouragement to you is to make tomorrow's to-do list tonight!

TAKEAWAY

When you wait to make your to-do list until the morning, what kind of emotions do you feel as you get started with your day? What about when you make your to-do list the night before? What differences, if any, do you notice about your emotional response in these two scenarios?

_____

_____

_____

_____

_____

_____

_____

_____

_____

_____

37

KNOW THYSELF

St. Augustine famously said, "Know thyself."

What type of a leader are you? One of the most important things you can do for the health and benefit of the ministry you lead is to know yourself. Do you understand your SHAPE for ministry? SHAPE is a wonderful acronym—it stands for Spiritual Gifts, Heart, Abilities, Personality, and Experiences. To know how you should lead your ministry, you must start by knowing yourself and your SHAPE.

Spiritual Gifts

Do you know what your spiritual gifts are? At the time of conversion, when a person truly becomes a Christian, God mystically endows them with spiritual gifts. These gifts act as a silver lining of sorts around your life. The Holy Spirit empowers someone in a very unique way, and provides a person who is using their gifts with an extra measure of grace and favor. What spiritual gifts has God given you?

Heart

What are you passionate about? If you have a passion for children, you've likely found yourself in children's ministry. Do you have a passion for the elderly? What about a passion for children who have no shoes, or who are left without a coat? Do you have a passion for refugees who find themselves in a new country? Knowledge of the things you are passionate about is a critical key to understanding your SHAPE for ministry.

Abilities

I believe there's a difference between spiritual gifts and abilities. I have abilities that don't have that spiritual sense around them. For example, I have the ability to play electric guitar. I don't believe, however, that I have the spiritual gift of music. Knowing the difference between your spiritual gifts and your abilities influences the ministry opportunities you are best suited for, and therefore the ones you pursue.

One of the most important things you can do for the health and benefit of the ministry you lead is to know yourself.

Personality

Are you an extrovert or an introvert? Many church leaders are afraid that God can't use an introverted person in a staff position at a local church. Nothing is further from the truth! An extrovert gains energy from being around people, while an introvert gains energy from times of solitude. Simply put, this distinction is about whether or not being around people charges or depletes you. I've seen many wonderful, introverted leaders excel at ministry. It just comes down to knowing yourself.

Experiences

The final stop on discovering your SHAPE in ministry is experiences. Any and every experience can be leveraged by God for His Kingdom. You just have to think about how. Are you a stay-at-home mom? There are plenty of opportunities to be positively used in ministry. Do you have abilities as a mid-level executive? Those experiences can and should influence how you lead in the local church. Have you ever had a broken arm? That pain doesn't need to be wasted in the Lord. Your ministry can be shaped by any and every experience that you've had.

Knowing yourself helps you to more fully understand how you can lead. Take time to write down, on a piece of paper, your SHAPE for ministry. After you know that, you can unleash yourself for new opportunities in the kingdom.

TAKEAWAY

What's your SHAPE? On the next page, write any insights you glean from the five categories above. What do these reveal about the way God designed you, and the ministry opportunities you're best suited for?

_____

_____

_____

_____

_____

_____

_____

_____

_____

_____

_____

_____

_____

_____

_____

_____

_____

_____

_____

Get Organized

Retain Volunteers

Avoid Burnout

38

LEADING...BUT NO ONE IS FOLLOWING

If you think you're leading, and yet no one is following, you may just be taking a walk.

Emotional intelligence is a key characteristic in any leadership role. Understanding people, and the ways they follow (or don't follow) your leadership, is a critical role in ministry especially. A leader needs to have that intuitive, gut-level sense of whether people are with you. Are they behind you? Or are they merely tolerating you? Do people want to hear from you? Do they ask with excitement about what's coming up next in your ministry? Or are people consistently questioning and criticizing what you are doing?

Just because you're in a leadership position doesn't mean you are a leader. Positional leadership is the lowest form of leadership. Emotional leadership— leading from a position of charisma and authenticity—is a higher, more effective form. If you think people are going to follow you wholeheartedly just because of your role, you're setting yourself up to be sorely disappointed.

Gather a team of people around you who are willing to share the honest truth with you.

Anybody can be hired; few can truly lead. There have been times when I've been self-deceived into thinking that people were hanging on my every word and anticipating my every move. Unfortunately, I was mistaken. I didn't have the sharp emotional intelligence to see that I'd lost some edge. Just because I'd successfully led in the past didn't mean people were still following me at that moment. The last thing I want to do as a leader is take the next hill, reach the top, and realize that I am completely alone.

Gather a team of people who are willing to share the honest truth with you. I once had a leader in my ministry who had been with me for over 10 years. We developed such a fantastic relationship that she was able and willing to tell me where I was missing the mark—when people were grumbling or questioning what we were doing as a ministry. That kind of counsel is invaluable to a leader.

Do you have trusted people who will let you know that you are wearing the Emperor's Clothes? You know this story, right? The emperor had such a poor understanding of himself that he found himself naked in front of his entire court, and nobody had the heart to tell him. Do you have someone around you who is willing to share the uncomfortable truth? Do you have somebody who will let you know when you are not being followed? We as leaders can often become self-deceived in our opinions about our abilities. If you think you are leading but no one is following, you are just taking a walk.

TAKEAWAY

Who are the select few voices in your ministry that you've allowed to speak truth into your leadership? Does anyone need to be added to this list? How do each of these individuals make you a better leader?

_____

_____

_____

_____

_____

_____

_____

_____

_____

39

SMILE MORE

One of the most important leadership principals that we can ever adopt is simply to smile more.

Now, if you are a librarian, my apologies, but I have a concept that I call a "Yes Face" and a "Librarian Face." The "Yes Face" is someone who displays a vibrant and inviting expression. Their face lights up, and you feel safe to ask them a question or say hello to them. On the contrary, the "Librarian Face" is a sour, pursed-lip expression—it sends the message that the person may snap if you ask them the wrong question (or any question, for that matter).

Now, some librarians are very helpful and joyful, so of course this characterization isn't always accurate. However, when I was recruiting volunteers, I always looked for Yes Faces. That volunteer could be the first experience a new family has at our church. Those visitors need to see a Yes Face!

**People want to be around a smiling face, and they
shy away from a frowning, brooding face.**

Let's say that I, as a senior leader of our church, have a constant scowl on my face during Sunday morning—I'm just brooding around trying to solve problems. How hard would it be, even while trying to solve problems, to adopt a Yes Face? Can I adopt a joyful smile? A welcoming expression? After all, heaven awaits! I have a job that serves in the ministry of God's Kingdom! Yes, it's hard; but I'm laying up treasure in heaven. Regardless of what's going on during the Sunday morning chaos, having a smile on your face is a profound win for you. People want to be around a smiling face, and they shy away from a frowning, brooding face.

Have you ever been around someone whose expression or demeanor has you asking them often, "Is everything okay?" They seem perpetually disturbed, upset, or impatient. If you have a grumpy face and you're crabby in your outlook, people are *not* going to want to be around you. But if you wear a Yes Face, and make an effort to be a joyful leader, you are inviting people to be a part of what your ministry has going on—and they *will* want to be a part of it!

My encouragement is this: smile more. Of course, we've all heard the research; it takes a certain number of facial muscles to frown and a certain number to smile. Who cares? At the end of the day, it's more appealing, more loving, and more inviting to smile. You will get farther in a leadership role by smiling.

TAKEAWAY

Besides smiling, think of 2-3 more tangible ways that you can exhibit a joyful, inviting demeanor. How can you exercise these things even in the face of problems or stresses that come along with your ministry role?

_____

_____

_____

_____

_____

_____

_____

_____

_____

_____

_____

_____

40

THE BEST PATH FORWARD IS A GREAT HISTORY

If you're new to ministry, you want to begin creating a wonderful history of excellence and execution. When you start your job, the last thing you want to do is to create for your employer a memory bank of less-than-excellent work. You want to dominate right from the beginning.

A reputation is earned through this formula: **Time + Consistency of Behavior = Reputation**

If you want to have a great future, it starts with having a fantastic track record. I see so many leaders desiring to do great things and having great ideas. However, their past failings and their historical inability to execute leaves them massively inhibited. An executive pastor or supervisor will have a massive dose of skepticism surrounding a leader's competence and ability when they see a poor history.

The last thing you want to do is create for your employer a memory bank of less than excellent work. You want to dominate right from the beginning.

How do you get beyond this? It's easy: you dominate every task you're handed, from the very start. Some of you may be reading this after you've been on the job for a while—you can think of some performance mistakes that you've made in the past. If you have a track record of dropping balls and failing at executing tasks, you have some hurdles to overcome. The best way forward is a brand new history.

Begin to rewrite your own personal ministry history with the next great thing you do. If you don't start rewriting your history, you're going to continue to have road blocks—you won't be given budget, opportunity, or a chance to succeed.

You need your supervisor to give you rope. Two things can happen with that rope: you can tie your very own noose that chokes you, or you can tie several knots in that rope and pull yourself towards success with your vision. Those knots become rungs on a rope ladder. Your leaders will see the history of how you've dominated and brought together a powerful ministry from your ideas. The choice is yours.

At the end of the day, the best future comes from a history of excellence.

TAKEAWAY

What are a few "knots" you can tie in your rope right now—those small, steady actions that will help you build a history of excellence?

_____

_____

_____

_____

_____

_____

_____

_____

_____

_____

_____

_____

41

THOSE WHO SAY AND THOSE WHO DO

I've often heard leaders share at length, droning on and on, about what they'd like to see happen...and yet, those items never come to fruition. These ideas never see the light of day, and we never get to see them executed. Before long, those who follow such leaders begin to take him or her leader less and less seriously.

When the leader boldly shares about a vision but there is never any follow through, everyone around the table slowly begins to put the car into neutral and just coast along. They know that, most likely, this new initiative will probably to nothing—their leader is all talk and little execution.

I want to be an individual who's long on vision *and* high on execution. The team you lead wants to be motivated—they want to spend their one and only life accomplishing something. When your leadership team is low on execution, they'll become disengaged and even lose respect for you! There's a difference between those who say and those who do. Frankly, you can differentiate these two kinds of individuals very quickly by asking, "Is something getting done, or is it all talk?"

**I want to be an individual who's long on
vision *and* high on execution.**

Don't be an individual who simply shares an idea and seeks to get others excited about it, but doesn't have the capacity or willpower to pull it off. No one will take this kind of leader seriously. Don't come to your team with fantastic-sounding ideas but no plan to make them a reality! It would be much better to share nothing than to share and show no follow through.

Be an individual who does what you say you'll do. There is a difference between those who say and those who do—and it's simply what gets done!

TAKEAWAY

Just like we talked about sharing the right amount in "Promise Little, Produce Much," this lesson covers the other side of the coin: getting things done. What are some practical ways you can ensure that your team feels motivated and equipped to carry out your vision—from the moment you first share it with them?

_____

_____

_____

_____

_____

_____

_____

_____

_____

_____

_____

_____

_____

_____

_____

_____

_____

_____

_____

VOLUNTEER
DEVELOPMENT

42

THE MOST POWERFUL FORM OF RECRUITING

The most powerful form of recruiting is done in person.

Right before Bill Hybels, from Willow Creek Church in Chicago, took the stage at a national children's ministry conference, I thought to myself, "Wow, it must be easy to work at a church this large! Think of all of the volunteers you'd have to choose from." About three minutes into Bill's keynote address, however, he said to us, "You may be sitting there thinking, "It would be easy to work at this church!"

He read my mind...and went on to explain that what I thought was the furthest thing from the truth. The larger the church, the more challenging it is to find volunteers. At the end of the day, no matter what your church size, true and effective volunteer recruiting comes down to relationships. In a large, ever-growing church, it's more difficult, in many ways, to develop substantive, significant relationships with individuals. No matter whether you serve at a small church with a limited volunteer pool, or a large church where your volunteer pool is larger but relationships are limited, recruitment is a challenging undertaking.

At the end of the day, no matter what your church size, true and effective volunteer recruiting comes down to relationships.

After serving as a children's director for over ten years, I have found many strategies that work for recruiting volunteers (and even more strategies that *don't* work!). For example, having the senior pastor make an impassioned plea to "get involved in children's ministry" usually results in absolutely nothing. Having an atrium display with banners, posters, and pamphlets also wasn't effective. Sending out that mass email to all of the parents asking them to respond with their ideal serving times had little results.

That day, Bill Hybels shared what I had already found to be true in my own ministry: nothing replaces a tap on the shoulder. Volunteering, at its core, is relationship building. I need to go out, interact with, engage with, and develop relationships with people. Out of the overflow of those relationships, I can share a compelling vision with them—an invitation to follow me into a deeper experience of God's grace, with God's people, to serve the church.

It all comes down to you personally asking someone to participate in the ministry—it comes down to a one-on-one conversation. Get to know people, take them to coffee or lunch, and ask what God is doing in their lives. Find out about their unique gifts and abilities. See if they are a good potential fit for your ministry area. You may think you don't have time for this; but I've learned that I don't have time to waste my efforts on strategies that don't work. If I'm going to spend my time, I want to spend it in the way that's most effective.

Of all the ways you can seek to engage and enlist a group of people to become volunteers, nothing produces effective results like a tap on the shoulder.

TAKEAWAY

Think about one or two people in your congregation who seem like good potential fits for your ministry. What are a few simple ideas for how you can connect with them this week, and get to know them better?

_____

_____

_____

_____

_____

43

UNDERUTILIZATION OF KEY VOLUNTEERS

We often think that the worst possible scenario we can bring about as a leader is to overwork a zealous volunteer. We definitely need to be cautious about this; but there is something just as detrimental: the underutilization of a key volunteer.

Years ago, I took over a large, established event at our church that had been in existence for quite a few years. This event brought 6,000 people into our church over the span of three days—and it found its way under my leadership. I'll never forget walking up to a key volunteer—a small business owner and top-tier contributor in so many areas of the church. Anyone would have loved to have this woman on their roster. I approached her with a simple question: "Would you be willing to participate in this upcoming event?" She folded her arms, lifted her chin, and said, "I will *never* volunteer at this event. Ever."

People want to use their gifts. They want to feel as if they are making a contribution. They don't want to do something weak and meaningless.

I took on the difficult, pastoral responsibility of asking why. Her reply was filled with hurt and frustration. "You guys got up on stage and begged for volunteers two years ago. You said you were in desperate need of people to help. I cleared my schedule, and showed up. When I arrived at the door, I checked in at the volunteer station, and was told that I wasn't needed." Another volunteer at the check-in desk told this woman that she could stand by a door and make sure that no one exited through it—just to give her something to do.

My heart sunk. This dear woman was a high-capacity volunteer, but had been handed a less-than-engaging job. People want to use their gifts. They want to feel as if they're making a significant contribution. They don't want to do something weak and meaningless.

If we in ministry are handing high-capacity volunteers low-end jobs, no wonder they don't feel fulfilled! It should come as no surprise that they don't want to participate any longer. Underutilization of volunteers is riskier than overworking someone. People want to work—so give them something hard to do and watch them surpass your expectations.

TAKEAWAY

What are some indicators of a "high-capacity" volunteer? What are some examples of "low-end" jobs that would make these individuals feel underutilized or even frustrated?

_____

_____

_____

_____

_____

_____

_____

_____

_____

_____

_____

_____

_____

44

VULNERABILITY IS THE KEY TO COMMUNITY

Everybody wants community. We were created for it. Isolation is one of the worst forms of punishment that a human being can endure. That's why solitary confinement is torture to inmates who undergo it. In community, we find beauty and health and healing. If community is a beautiful treasure—a prize behind a locked door—the key to get into that treasure-filled room is vulnerability.

Now, vulnerability is a hard thing for any of us to exhibit. To be vulnerable means you're putting yourself into a position of defenselessness—a position to be hurt. You are opening yourself up to being hurt when you're honest and transparent about your failings, your flaws, and your fears.

I've sat under leaders who had such a fear of transparency that they created elaborate structures around themselves to ensure that their perfect persona was always in place. Even when it was quite clear that they'd made a mistake, they'd call up that quick façade. Everyone under the authority of such a leader knew better. Their trust would have gone through the roof, if only the leader had admitted that they were human—that they needed grace. We all would have extended grace! But they didn't feel safe enough, or understand the beauty of true community enough, to let down their walls.

I want to love as if there is no risk of being hurt.

Shifting our focus to your role as a leader, in ministry and beyond, consider what a gift it would be to those you serve if you were vulnerable! What if you could articulate your failings, your flaws, and your fears? What if you expressed them freely, being secure enough in your identity in Christ to be transparent with others?

People would see your humanity and hunger to follow such an authentic, vulnerable leader. Is there a risk? Absolutely. Could someone exploit your honesty and seek to do damage when you're at your most vulnerable? Well, the answer is yes. However, I want to love as if there is no risk of being hurt.

The key to community is vulnerability.

TAKEAWAY

What's one flaw, failing, or weakness that you could be vulnerable with your team about? What freedom might this bring to your team in sharing their own weaknesses and vulnerabilities? Can you recall any times in Christ's life when He was vulnerable with the disciples about His own humanity?

_____

_____

_____

_____

_____

_____

_____

_____

_____

_____

_____

_____

_____

_____

_____

_____

_____

45

DELEGATION MUST INCLUDE DETAILS

Have you ever handed off a project to a volunteer with little or no instruction? Do you delegate duties simply based on whether or not your volunteers are willing to accept them? There's a difference between delegating and dumping. Handing projects off to another person without providing clear details and direction may feel like delegation, but in reality, it's just dumping. Handing off projects without coaching is like essence pulling up a dump truck and offloading a huge volume of tasks on an unsuspecting individual. Are you in the practice of dumping? Or do you truly delegate?

Delegation must include direction and details in order for your volunteers to succeed. The *how* and *why* of each task needs to be explained. Does an individual know the values upon which your ministry runs? Do they know the rationale and reasoning behind this specific task—why it's important? If you want to create a long-term relationship with individuals who execute large tasks for you, it will come down to your ability to provide details rather than merely dumping. True delegation involves relationship, as well as providing the systematic pathways and processes by which an individual will complete tasks.

Delegation must include direction and details in order for your volunteers to succeed.

Years ago, I read a book about having a virtual assistant. Your support staff could live a world away, but perform tasks for you with nothing but digital instructions to guide them. This book spent an inordinate amount of time explaining how the success of your virtual assistant is in direct relation to the amount of detail you provide for them. The likelihood of talking to a virtual assistant on the phone or seeing them face to face is low, so tons of details need to be provided to help them understand what's being asked of them. Whether you're working with a volunteer a world away, or one right next door to you, your ability to hand them detailed and descriptive directions is vital (not to mention courteous).

Don't dump on your volunteers. Help them succeed by giving them clear direction. Take an extra 30-45 minutes and articulate the details, direction, and description of what you need done and why. You'll be grateful you did.

TAKEAWAY

Think of one or two of the most common tasks you assign to your volunteers/assistants. How could you improve upon the amount of detail you give to your support team about these tasks?

_____

_____

_____

_____

_____

_____

_____

_____

_____

_____

_____

_____

_____

46

DON'T OVERSELL THE SACRIFICE

When recruiting, don't oversell the sacrifice. Simply share the opportunity you're offering to volunteers to make an impact in the kingdom of God. So many leaders walk into the recruiting conversation apologetic and sheepish. They feel like they are a bad person, taking something away from this potential volunteer. As they present their ideas, they feel as if they're robbing the other person of time and energy.

These leaders may say things like, "I know this is a burden to you, but..." or, "I know you're super busy and have tons going on, however..." Don't open the conversation with a weak, pathetic position. Understand that you're providing someone an opportunity, with their one and only life, to lay up treasure in heaven—NOT burdening them by asking them to serve. You are allowing your team members an opportunity to serve in the Kingdom of God and to influence believers (or nonbelievers!) for eternity. That's no small undertaking! You're not *taking* anything from them at all—you're investing in them!

What would happen if you simply changed your recruitment language from a negative posture to an opportunistic posture? When you frame a volunteer opportunity as a chance to lay up treasure in heaven, your efforts go significantly further than if you come into the conversation with an attitude of burden. You are not a burden to those you lead. You're the leader. You frame the conversation. Frame it in the positive, and don't oversell the sacrifice.

What would happen if you simply changed your recruitment language from a negative posture to an opportunistic posture?

Not only are you inviting them into an opportunity to make an impact in the Kingdom of God—you're also inviting them into an opportunity for community.

If your ministry is set up in a healthy way, new volunteers will be rubbing shoulders with other, experienced leaders. These are the things you can showcase as opportunities and wins to potential team members.

Another way to showcase opportunity is by using the marketing concept of scarcity. Rather than saying, "We have ten roles to fill," try saying, "We only have ten opportunities left." That simple word change allows a volunteer to see that they might not be able to receive one of these roles. They could miss out! Say, "We only have three opportunities left to be a small group leader this year. I know we're going to fill them, and I want to provide you an opportunity to be a part of this team." This lets the potential volunteer think about missing out on that amazing opportunity, and decide whether that's something they're willing to risk.

Choose your language wisely. Don't oversell the sacrifice. Overshare the opportunity that your recruits have to impact the Kingdom of God.

TAKEAWAY

What's one simple way you can change the phrasing that you use when speaking to potential volunteers or team members—how can you make it more positive and opportunity-oriented?

_____

_____

_____

_____

_____

_____

_____

_____

_____

47

PEOPLE STAY WHERE THEY HAVE SAY

As a leader, it's important to understand that gaining input from those you lead helps them to feel that they are part of your vision. When your team gives input, they are helping to shape the future of your ministry. Giving people a say will give *them* a desire to stay.

I have to admit, however, that I struggle to do this. Maybe you have the same problem. I want to control how things go. I don't want to listen to a volunteer who may have an idea about changing the ministry. However, allowing your volunteers to have a voice in the ministry, difficult though it may be, allows them to have a deeper sense of ownership. "Diplomacy is the art of letting someone else have your way." These wise words came to me from the most unexpected, unlikely of places: a Chinese fortune cookie. At the end of the day, we as leaders can shape the way a conversation is carried out so that people end up desiring to go in the direction that we've already predetermined.

Allowing your volunteers to have a voice in the ministry, difficult though it may be, allows them to have a deeper sense of ownership.

Now, this may sound like a manipulative method of leadership. It certainly can be, but keep in mind that manipulation is a condition of the heart. Start with a sincere heart of leadership and a desire to do and lead great things—then, gather a team around you and invite them to carry out the vision with you. It all comes down to communication—to sharing your vision while soliciting feedback and input. Leaders need to be excellent listeners, while still staying in line with where you want to go.

There are people in your ministry who have far greater gifts and abilities than you do. They lead in the marketplace. They have degrees that surpass your personal level of expertise. For us not to include them in the future of our ministry is foolish. While you are the one in the driver's seat, allow others to influence the direction you go. People stay where they have a say. Give people an opportunity to influence the ministry you lead.

TAKEAWAY

Can you think of any decisions or initiatives in your ministry that would benefit from others' input and expertise? What kinds of questions can you ask in this area to invite feedback without surrendering your place in the driver's seat?

_____

_____

_____

_____

_____

_____

_____

_____

_____

_____

_____

_____

_____

_____

_____

_____

48

CREATING RELATIONSHIP *WITH* VOLUNTEERS AND *BETWEEN* VOLUNTEERS

Years ago, I was sadly surprised when I found out that some of our key volunteers, who had been serving as small group leaders for 40 weeks of the school year, didn't know the name of the leaders sitting right next to them. I was abhorrently disappointed in my own leadership—how could two individuals who sat ten feet apart from one another for 40 consecutive Sundays not know each other's names?

It was a reality that pointed to something painfully true about my leadership — I wasn't creating opportunities for volunteers to get to know one another. Of course, we stressed that we wanted volunteers to know the *kids* in their small group — their names, passions, sporting events, and so on. But we hadn't provided ample opportunity for volunteers to get to know one another.

**We as ministry leaders have to find ways for our
leaders to connect with us and with one another.**

Granted, I was making my way around the room to get to know all of these volunteers personally. That's a fantastic start. But I found that a greater level of relational victory was achieved when volunteers knew one another. People want to be in community, and serving should lead to a greater sense of community. We weren't providing an opportunity for that to take place. The way our team sought to solve this problem was by creating volunteer family gatherings once or twice a quarter at someone's house. These gatherings included family members, and were quite well attended. We went so far as to host volunteer gatherings on a Friday *and* Saturday evening to accommodate schedules.

It took a lot of work, but we figured out ways to scale this opportunity. We created meals that could be easily stored from Friday to Saturday. We had crock pots filled with taco meat, or a soup night where we could save the soup one night to the next. We had sign-ups for people to bring food. I can't begin to tell you how important this was to the health of our ministry. Volunteers got to know one another, sit by one another at dinner, and introduce their kids to one another. Volunteers were no longer these isolated entities missing out on relationships with other adults.

Part of the fear — and sometimes an unintended consequence — of serving is that you miss out on adult relationships. We as ministry leaders have to find ways for our leaders to connect with us and with one another. These volunteer dinners did so much good. We found people rearranging their schedules to ensure that they could attend. We even had backyard barefoot kickball tournaments. These volunteer gatherings turned into an event nobody wanted to miss. My encouragement to you, in your ministry context, is to find ways for volunteers to connect with one another.

TAKEAWAY

What are some simple ideas for ways to introduce, and foster relationships among, your volunteers? Look online and ask your ministry friends for ideas!

_____

_____

_____

_____

_____

_____

_____

_____

49

SIMPLY SAY THANKS

It blows my mind how many leaders don't understand the value of appreciation. Appreciation can come in many forms, but I want to speak right now to simply saying thank you. It's a simple phrase we were taught at a very young age. Over the years, I've been completely stunned at the power of those two words.

When I first started in children's ministry, I inherited a team of weary, burned out, cranky volunteers. They were frustrated, furious, and fed up—they wanted to quit. When I took the job, I made it a personal challenge to handwrite a thank you note to every single person serving at every single layer of the ministry. I did this by creating thank you cards, printing off scores of address labels, and writing two postcards a week until the job was done.

My team and I would systematically send handwritten cards to all volunteers. and even to our church elders. Interestingly enough, I came back to my office one day to find a voicemail from a key volunteer—someone had been crabby and rather caustic in the past. When I heard her name on the message, I cringed—what kind of attack would she level at me today? However, she burst into tears of thanksgiving and joy. She said, "In all of my years of serving in children's ministry, no one has ever said thank you to me. I received your postcard. Thank you so much for taking the time to simply say thank you."

**Consider calling someone who served in your ministry
area last week, and simply say thank you to them.**

Her statement claiming that no one had ever thanked her may or may not have been true. But quite possibly, no one had ever said thank you to her in a way that *mattered*—that reached her heart—until that point.

Can I give you a challenge? You may think sending a handwritten postcard to every volunteer is a lofty goal—and it might be. Could I encourage you to consider calling someone who served in your ministry area last week, and simply say thank you to them? Call them for a reason other than to require something of them. What if you made a phone call that only said "Thank you?"

The power of thank you is an untold blessing. Remember those words that we were taught as children. Simply say thank you.

TAKEAWAY

Today, think of one or two personalized ways you can thank your volunteers, and make a plan or schedule for how you'll say thank you to each one of them in this next season. Remember, these ways can be simple!

_____

_____

_____

_____

_____

_____

_____

_____

_____

_____

_____

_____

_____

50

HURT PEOPLE HURT PEOPLE

I've been alive, and in ministry, for long enough to understand that when someone hurts another person, it's often because they themselves are hurting.

In a ministry context, I have found time and time again that, when someone seeks to hurt you as the pastor, there is often something else going on. The issue you're facing is often *not* the underlying issue. Hurt people literally hurt people. Everyone is hurting. We've got deep wounds inside us. It's to your advantage, as a pastor, to understand that everyone is coming to your door with injuries. Sometimes, the most painful experiences I've had are those that come about because of deeply hurt people.

I can cut a lot of slack and give a lot of grace when I realize that an injured person inadvertently seeks to injure others. I don't take it as personally. Many years ago, I learned a very valuable, very difficult lesson: Being a shepherd in the Kingdom of God means that sometimes, the sheep will bite you, and it will hurt. It can hurt to have an injured, emotionally-pained sheep who, on the outside, looks perfect, but who is wounded inside. They see you, their shepherd, as someone to lash out at. This has happened to me; and if it hasn't happened to you, it's only a matter of time.

Being a shepherd in the Kingdom of God means that sometimes, the sheep will bite you, and it will hurt.

Hurt people hurt people. I encourage you, with all of my heart, to give grace. Often, it's a simple act of psychological displacement. When someone is walking through their living room and they're upset about something completely different, they may kick a piece of furniture, or even—God forbid—the dog. That is displacement. The dog didn't do anything wrong, but their anger and frustration has been pent up long enough that somebody is going to be on the receiving end of it.

Pastor, you are going to be on the receiving end of hurt people. Jesus Christ said that He came for the sick, not the healthy. We are in spiritual urgent care, meaning polished-looking people are often deeply injured. They will take that out on us. After all, we're an easy target. While I don't think this condones anyone's behavior (people ought to be held accountable for un-Christ-like behavior), you need to have a free grace card to not take it personally.

Hurt people hurt people. Controlling people are wounded and scared. Yes, the sheep bite. The role of a shepherd is to lead the sheep beside quiet waters, into green pastures, and to care for them.

Sheep are interesting animals. Let's imagine that a herd is grazing quietly, the sun is out, not a cloud in the sky, and one sheep bends down to eat a tuft of grass and a blade of grass goes up its nose. The sheep quickly rears its head back. Now, that action should not cause alarm. However, sheep are easily scared beings. The heard freaks out and thinks there must be danger nearby—and makes a run for it. Even the sheep that had a blade of grass go up its nose scurries off with the rest. This is called herd mentality. Sheep are scared, and the whole herd will follow each other, even to their own deaths.

What does this mean for us as leaders? Well, you don't want to scare the sheep. Let's imagine you are going to bring forth some change in your ministry. There is a way to do this that is going to comfort the flock, and there is a way to that is going to scare the living daylights out of them. They might just run off a cliff! Human beings have a threshold for change—they can only take so much. If you constantly change everything in your ministry, you might want to think about pushing pause and giving your sheep a little rest—an opportunity to acclimate to the changes you've made so far.

Not only do sheep scare easily, but moms and dads with small children scare easily. Moms and dads are hardwired to think about and protect their children at all costs. They desire the best for their children; and when they think their children are in danger or are somehow being short-changed or slighted, they get scared. Their response can come across as angry, hostile, or enraged. When one person has a negative, adverse reaction to your ministry, that person can rear their head and cause many others to think that there is danger where there really is no danger at all.

Don't scare the sheep. Be a minister of peace and reconciliation. Understand that your role as a shepherd is to protect the sheep, sometimes even from themselves. Know that people hurt people, and that there is usually an underlying reason behind people's tone, words, and actions.

TAKEAWAY

How does the example of sheep and a shepherd help reframe your view of how you relate to those in your ministry? Are there any "difficult" volunteers or families who may be going through some hard circumstances at the moment? How might this be affecting their tone towards you?

Get Organized

Retain Volunteers

Avoid Burnout

51

IDENTIFY THE FAITHFUL FEW

Identify the faithful few in your ministry and invite them into greater involvement.

There are many categories of people you serve with in your ministry area. Can you identify some of the individuals you can call to greater levels of involvement? Before you identify the faithful few, let's take a step back and look at the ministry of Jesus—the levels of people He chose to invite into His life.

There were many people following Christ that He had an influence on. Some of these people, however, were a part of Jesus's inner circle, His closest group. It's interesting that Jesus had one individual closer to Him than the rest—John. John refers to himself as "the disciple whom Jesus loved." When special things were happening, John was always present. At the Last Supper, John leaned into Jesus, rested on His chest, and asked "Lord, who is the one who will betray you?" Jesus didn't tell that answer to Bartholomew. He didn't tell it to Levi. He told it to John alone.

As Jesus was dying on the cross, He looked to John and said, "Behold, this is my mother. Mother, behold, this is your son." John was close to Jesus.

Now there was also a different group John was a part of—the main three: Peter, James, and John. This group was the next layer of people who found themselves close to Christ. When Jesus the time came for Jesus to go up onto the Mount of Transfiguration, it was Peter, James and John that he chose to accompany him. When He healed a sick daughter, He brought Peter, James and John. These individuals were at the epicenter of what Jesus was doing.

There was yet another group called "the Twelve." The twelve disciples were close to Jesus when He began to explain His parables. They were the chosen ones, who were given the Great Commission and who formed the beginnings of the church as we know it.

After "the Twelve," there was another group: the 72. The 72 were a group whom Jesus sent out two by two as He expanded His ministry. This group was special, chosen, and each given special instructions and jobs.

Identify people who are the faithful few, and call them to deeper layers of service.

Beyond this group was another called, "the following." Most people don't realize this, but there was a group of 120-150 people who were with Jesus on many occasions. This group included women and men. Evidence of this group includes Matthias, who was chosen to replace Judas. Matthias' qualifications indicate that he was with the disciples from the beginning. This group of people was not often called out by name. Still there was one last group: the masses, or the 5,000. This was a grand group of people who listened to Jesus, and yet they were only on the periphery.

In your ministry, have you identified the people who are in these categories? There individuals who know you as a ministry leader, yet they are not involved in your ministry—let's call these individuals "the Masses." There are "the 72"—those who are engaged in the ministry, and yet they're not your closest confidants. "The 12" are your core group—your inside crew. Within that group there should be a group of three who are your Peter, James, and John. These are the individuals to whom you throw out new ideas. They're on the inside, and they see the challenging aspects of your ministry.

Then there is "The John"—your most trusted ally. My question to you is, do these different layers exist within your ministry? Have you identified people who you could move from your 72 into a more prominent position in your 12? How would you go about doing that?

Start by identifying people who are excited about the ministry—who show up early, and have a general acumen for working in your area. Invite them into a closer, deeper layer of leadership with you. It's important to verbally call people to a greater level of engagement, and it can happen through a tap on the shoulder. Identify people who are the faithful few, and call them to deeper layers of service.

TAKEAWAY

Who are a few people in your "Masses" who may be able to move into the 72 group? What about members of the 72 group who can move into the 12? Who are your top three? Who is your John? What are a few practical ideas for inviting certain members to move up a layer?

_____

_____

_____

_____

_____

_____

_____

_____

_____

_____

_____

_____

_____

_____

_____

_____

_____

Get Organized

Retain Volunteers

Avoid Burnout

52

UNITY IS A KINGDOM VALUE

I believe unity is one of the most important things inside the local church. We need to be unified. Now, this can be difficult at times, to say the least. There have been occasions where, behind closed doors, I was vehemently opposed to a decision that the church was making. I had enough courage and relationship with my senior leaders that I would aggressively share my rationale for why I felt we should not move in a particular direction. Sometimes, we would modify the decision based on my input; sometimes we would not.

Moving out of that isolated back room of a leadership discussion, we would move into a more public arena, where the rest of the church would begin to think about and interact with the decisions we were making. Now, notice I didn't say the decisions *those leaders* were making." No—I made this decision with them behind closed doors. I didn't agree with it; but once that door opened up, I sought to be a united front. It was difficult, but essential.

There is nothing more toxic for the senior leader than another senior leader publically dismantling their idea.

There were times I had to articulate a vision with which I did not agree. There were times I heard people give the same argument I had given behind closed doors, and had to maintain my integrity and showcase a healthy, united front. I'm not a person who is robotically obedient. I think for myself and I operate quite independently. However, that doesn't mean I am going to tear down a decision in the public arena. That can't happen. There is nothing more toxic for the senior leader than another senior leader publically dismantling their idea.

Unity is a Kingdom value. If I don't get my way, can I still move forward and support the decision? I found myself, on many occasions, reluctantly saying yes. If, however, you find yourself unable to agree publically with the decisions being made, and you cannot keep up a united front with your senior leadership, it may be time for you to pray about transitioning out of that role.

There are seasons of life and seasons of ministry. If you can't get behind big-picture decisions that your church is making, it may be time for you to go. The church has no room for a divided house. It will fall. This is God's church, and the last thing you want to be is a cause of public disunity. You should be cautious and tread lightly.

Think for yourself, express your thoughts, earn the right to be heard. However, once a decision has been made, keep unity at all costs. Unity does not mean lying. Unity does not mean I turn off my brain and robotically repeat a set of phrases I've been told to say. I can use my creativity, my voice, and my logic; but I have to present a united front. Unity is a Kingdom value.

TAKEAWAY

Do you find it easy or difficult to publically support a church decision that you don't privately agree with? Why do you think this is? How do you practically go about promoting public unity when you don't agree with a decision?

_____

_____

_____

_____

_____

_____

_____

_____

CPSIA information can be obtained
at www.ICGtesting.com
Printed in the USA
BVHW040731270721
612359BV00005B/9